MW01069542

"Karen Moore is among the most innovative and strategic professionals in the communications industry and is setting a new standard for what advocacy means. With a true passion for advocacy, Karen empowers those who she interacts with in a tremendously thoughtful manner. Her ability to make connections with determination allows her to shape the conversation with engaged voices, leading the charge surrounding our most critical patient-access issues. Her insights and guidance are well recognized and sought after by individuals and organizations across the industry."

—Scott LaGanga, Senior Vice President of Advocacy and Strategic Alliances, Pharmaceutical Research and Manufacturers of America (PhRMA)

"As a nonpartisan organization that empowers women to be successful in the political arena, we understand that a thorough mastery of advocacy is a must-have. Karen Moore is the leader in successful advocacy how-to, from messaging, networking, and crisis communications to impactful strategies that help you unify your messages to be heard. She is consistently our highest-rated speaker and a true national expert who is a game changer for our advocacy programs."

—Rachel Michelin, Executive Director/CEO, California Women Lead

"When it comes to winning advocacy battles, Karen B. Moore is the undisputed leader. She is able to easily reach Hispanic audiences and move them to action, making a difference at every turn. Her in-depth knowledge of the target audience and the legislative process have been perfectly honed to serve organizations across the globe."

—Julio Fuentes, President,
Florida State Hispanic Chamber of Commerce

"Karen Moore is the top advocacy powerhouse. From impactful messaging to effective grassroots activities, she is the best in the business. Her strategies are powerful, and the results are guaranteed. If you could read only one book before engaging in advocacy, this is the must-read primer."

—Rene Rodriguez, MD, President,
Salud USA

"Karen Moore is a master communicator and connector, and in the world of advocacy, that's priceless. No one is better at bringing people together, educating and inspiring them, and leading them to achieve great things. As a nonprofit organization, we rely on partnerships to help us achieve our goals and communicate our issues, and Karen is an expert in developing and maintaining these strategic alliances."

—Michael Ruppal, Executive Director,
The AIDS Institute

behind the
RED DOOR

UNLOCK YOUR ADVOCACY
INFLUENCE AND SUCCESS

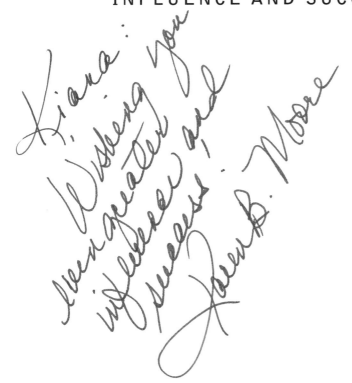

behind the

RED DOOR

UNLOCK YOUR ADVOCACY
INFLUENCE AND SUCCESS

KAREN B. MOORE

Major Contributor: Terrie Ard
Social Media Contributor: Scott Monty

Published by Advantage, Charleston, South Carolina.
Member of Advantage Media Group.

ADVANTAGE is a registered trademark and the Advantage colophon is a trademark of Advantage Media Group, Inc.

Printed in the United States of America.

ISBN: 978-1-59932-660-3
LCCN: 2016935784

This publication is designed to provide accurate and authoritative information in regard to the subject matter covered. It is sold with the understanding that the publisher is not engaged in rendering legal, accounting, or other professional services. If legal advice or other expert assistance is required, the services of a competent professional person should be sought.

Advantage Media Group is proud to be a part of the Tree Neutral® program. Tree Neutral offsets the number of trees consumed in the production and printing of this book by taking proactive steps such as planting trees in direct proportion to the number of trees used to print books. To learn more about Tree Neutral, please visit **www.treeneutral.com.** To learn more about Advantage's commitment to being a responsible steward of the environment, please visit **www.advantagefamily.com/green**

TreeNeutral

Advantage Media Group is a publisher of business, self-improvement, and professional development books and online learning. We help entrepreneurs, business leaders, and professionals share their Stories, Passion, and Knowledge to help others Learn & Grow. Do you have a manuscript or book idea that you would like us to consider for publishing? Please visit **advantagefamily.com** or call **1.866.775.1696.**

To my husband, Richard, the love of my life.

TABLE OF CONTENTS

ACKNOWLEDGMENTS

I am blessed to have had so many people help me on this book journey. A very special and sincere thank you to:

Terrie Ard, President, Moore Communications Group, the smartest and most strategic woman I have ever met. Her sage counsel and significant input into the writing of each chapter in this book was invaluable to its success.

Scott Monty, one of this country's top leaders in the digital/social world. Thank you for your perspective and insights into the ever-changing landscape. The chapter on social/digital media is better because of your thoughts.

Whitney Pickett, whose grace, enthusiasm, and smile have kept all things moving forward for me and Moore Communications Group. Her project management skills are a significant reason for this book's publication.

My **Moore Communications Group** family, working alongside you has been the greatest privilege I could ever ask for. Thank you to each one of you for your smart, dedicated focus on always doing the right thing, for the right reason, in the right way.

And none of this would be possible without my family, who encourages and supports me in so many ways:

Jarrod, our son, who brings me the greatest joy. Thank you for always being so supportive. You have grown and matured into such a generous and accomplished man.

*My precious parents, **Doug and Jean Batchelor**, who have encouraged me throughout every step of life's journey. You are my inspiration.*

*To my dearest sister and friend, **Cheryl Elias**, who inspires me each day. You and your wonderful husband, Bob, are a blessing to our family.*

A special thank you to all the extended family, friends, colleagues, and clients who have been helpful in providing advice, encouragement, and support. You have helped make the dream of writing this book a reality.

And to all the individual advocates and advocacy organizations who have stood up for the vulnerable and voiceless to make a positive change in this world.

INTRODUCTION

Why does the image of a red door have to do with advocacy? In feng shui, a red door signifies "welcome," a place where energy enters. In the American tradition, a red door signified a welcome place for those traveling on rural roads in their horse and buggy to find a night's rest, camaraderie, and open discussion. In fact, on the Underground Railroad, a red door signified a house as a place of refuge and safety.

To me, the red door is a differentiator. The color red means energy, strength, power, and passion. It means action. And if you take that strength and passion and incorporate it in a strategic advocacy engagement, you can turn it into action for your organization. So the red door strategies that I propose in this book, whether they're traditional or innovative, are the tools and tactics to help you create success in your advocacy efforts.

The Merriam-Webster Dictionary defines *advocacy* as "the act or process of supporting a cause or proposal."[1] But advocacy is being redefined. Advocacy is no longer just a tactic used in public affairs, but an essential part of any successful communication campaign. There's a rise not only at the local, state, and federal levels but also internationally. We're seeing advocacy groups working together to help shape public opinion and affect public policy. Today it's more than just a not-for-profit advocacy group organizing to storm Capitol Hill. It's more than just a well-financed business group that walks the

---

1 "Advocacy," *Merriam-Webster*, accessed December 29, 2015, http://www.merriam-webster.com/dictionary/advocacy.

halls of the capitol building once a month. It's collaboration between nontraditional allies who, even though they may not agree on everything, are coming together to accomplish mutually beneficial goals.

For instance, we have seen members of the pharmaceutical industry and cancer organizations and institutions join forces for the greater good. These groups may not always align in their mission, goals, and objectives but have worked together as a united force to address legislation surrounding cancer parity.

But advocacy is more than addressing public policy. It is now being brought into the workplace and into the overall marketing strategy. This has created what are known as internal and external advocates.

Externally, advocate initiatives are being cultivated and effectively deployed by the business community to gain market share, to influence buying decisions, or to protect or strengthen the corporate brand. A good example of this is the Ford Drive 4 UR School program. For every test drive taken, the Ford Motor Company donates $20 to a local school, up to $6,000.[2]

The rise in internal advocacy is also fascinating, with companies today working to create a culture of advocacy within their organizations. They're engaging and empowering individuals to support a cause by creating "brand ambassadors" and circles of influence to drive action.

Technology has made advocacy more accessible and more powerful. Social media has become a game changer in advocacy, in both the public and private sector. If your organization is not fully engaged in social media to support your business goals through advocacy, you are missing out on opportunities your competitors are leveraging.

---

2 Ford Motor Company, "Drive 4UR School," Last modified 2015, https://forddrive4ucom/.

Advocacy is now a necessary asset that should be used by every organization. Whether the priorities for an organization are to increase revenue and profit, engage in new markets, mitigate threats, enhance corporate brand, or affect public policy, advocacy can help accomplish those business goals.

THE POWER OF ADVOCACY

At Moore Communications Group (MCG), we focus on using advocacy to make a positive impact for our clients and our community. We use advocacy to help shape public opinion and policies, to sell products and services, to build conversations and communities, and more. In the field of health care, for example, we start by looking for ways to engage patients, physicians, health care providers, insurance leaders, policymakers, businesses, and nonprofits in an effort to find solutions that are in the best interest of the patient, while involving stakeholders in building a more effective and supportive ecosystem to have a positive impact on the whole health care infrastructure. For most advocacy campaigns, we begin by building a coalition or alliance of like-minded people to create an environment where discussions can be held to generate positive outcomes.

Each campaign begins by building the necessary architecture for a successful advocacy program by:

- defining the purpose of the campaign

- building and cultivating the brand

- bringing the right people to the table

- creating and mobilizing champions

- determining what activities in which to engage

- communicating tactics and strategies to stakeholders

- measuring success

I've been working in the field of advocacy for more than two decades, and I've seen advocacy undergo substantial changes over that time.

Before entering the advocacy arena, I worked as the director of marketing and public relations at two institutions of higher education. In time, I saw an opportunity to move into the private sector, so I opened a one-person public relations firm and landed my first client, a blood bank. The organization needed my help to identify and activate people to sign up for the National Marrow Donor Program in an effort to help a young child in need. I had to determine whom we should talk to, what tools we should use, how we could leverage existing assets, and how we could amplify our voice in order to encourage people to sign up.

The campaign had to be implemented in a very short time because that child was in intensive care and needed a bone marrow transplant right away. So in less than a week, we created a regional campaign to activate people to sign up for the National Marrow Donor Program. Within one day, we had more people sign up for the registry than in any previous year. It was exciting to feel that we might actually be able to save the life of a child, and it was done by utilizing public relations, marketing, advertising, and grassroots and grasstops advocacy engagement. The campaign was composed of an army of volunteers and a variety of tools put together in a strategic way to communicate the message to people that their participation could save a person's life while improving the quality of life in our community and across the nation.

That first campaign showed me how powerful the voice of an advocate could be. It showed me how building a campaign to help a vulnerable segment of the population could bring attention to issues and get people to take action and solve a problem. Sadly, we did not find a match, and that brave little boy lost his battle, but we did find matches to help others.

Since then, I have fostered that passion for advocacy at MCG. Every day, I go home knowing that the work our team does helps make this world a better place.

I started MCG because I believed that I could give a voice to people who are voiceless. I had a passion for seeing how we could help businesses succeed, and I knew there were resources out there that could be utilized better and that advocacy should be one of those resources. Whether an organization is shaping public policy or selling products, what I've experienced over the past twenty-plus years is that, when advocacy is done well, it is extremely powerful and successful.

In addition to my expertise in advocacy, I've included insights from Terrie Ard, a communications and branding expert and president at MCG, and Scott Monty, an internationally recognized leader in digital communications, digital transformation, and marketing.

This book is designed to help decision makers and others understand why advocacy is a vital tool for their organization, regardless of their specific industry. I'm going to walk you through a comprehensive look at advocacy including building an advocacy plan, creating and utilizing a brand, building and mobilizing internal and external stakeholders, using digital/social media, dealing with crisis communications, and finally, measuring results.

Ultimately, there are three things I'd like you to take away from this book: (1) the understanding that advocacy is a tool that can help you accomplish your business objectives, (2) advocacy is a very powerful opportunity that you should be leveraging, and (3) if you're not leveraging advocacy and using it effectively, then you're leaving assets on the table. Advocacy can help you build influence and achieve success. Think of advocacy as a way to give a bigger, louder voice to your organization, brand, or issue.

CHAPTER 1

WHY ADVOCACY?

Never doubt that a small group of thoughtful, committed citizens can change the world. Indeed, it's the only thing that ever has.
—Margaret Mead

Advocacy should be a required asset for any organization trying to make its mark on the world. Done well, advocacy can further your organization's efforts to achieve its goals and objectives, and it should be a resource in every toolbox.

Just what is advocacy? What was once considered an effective tool for nonprofits' voices to be heard on Capitol Hill has evolved into a major collaborative effort of organizations and nontraditional allies of every size and focus to effect change.

To clarify further, let me demonstrate the difference between advocacy and marketing. According to *The Merriam-Webster Dictionary*, *advocacy* is "the act or process of supporting a cause or proposal,"[3] whereas *marketing* is defined as "the activities that are involved in making people aware of a company's products."[4] According to those definitions, if you take a picture and put it on social media, that's marketing. But if you attach a belief to your action, such as every child should have breakfast, then you've also engaged in advocacy.

You must also understand the importance of internal and external advocates. We'll talk about these powerful components of any advocacy campaign in the chapters ahead, but for now, internal advocacy is about rallying your own employees to become your champions for making change, whether it's addressing a specific issue or changing public policy. External advocacy is about collaborating with others to create allies to accomplish a similar goal. Whether internal or external, the best advocates are those who have a great story to tell, the people who can talk about why an issue is very personal to them and why it's important for them to see this change take place. So whether they are patients able to speak from a personal perspective of why a public policy change should occur or they are employees supporting the company's commitment to corporate responsibility, the people who have a passion or personal connection to the cause are the best to champion it. When you combine these two types of advocates—internal and external—you take your efforts to an entirely new level to adopt a more integrated approach.

---

3 "Advocacy," *Merriam-Webster*.
4 "Marketing," *Merriam-Webster*, accessed December 30, 2015, http://www.merriam-webster.com/dictionary/marketing.

What we're seeing today is a significant blurring of the line between traditional marketing and what has long been known as advocacy. Instead of marketing and advocacy being distinctly separate activities, many organizations are finding ways to straddle the line between the two.

A good example of this is Kellogg's and its wonderful campaign called Share Your Breakfast™. The company engaged advocates through social media and assigned a dollar value to each level of participation.[5] For every participant who shared a breakfast description or photo on Kellogg's Facebook page or Twitter, the company donated funds to Action for Healthy Kids. Those funds were used to buy breakfasts for schoolchildren. The goal of the campaign was to share one million breakfasts with kids who needed them. In this campaign, advocacy was not just about a corporation enhancing its brand with a positive message, but it was also about supporting a cause that people can rally around—in this case, hunger.

The beauty of the Kellogg's campaign was that it engaged people in the conversation to make change. It wasn't direct marketing in that it was asking consumers to buy a Kellogg's product. It was a conversation at a much higher level about childhood hunger in America. The campaign extended beyond sales of cereal to having conversations about issues of public opinion, and ideally, perhaps, of public policy.

Today brands such as Southwest Airlines are using employees to engage in social media and build brand advocates. For instance, the *NUTS about Southwest* blog is mostly the result of employee posts, people writing about their life at Southwest, activities of the team, and more. Different employees have been writing about their unique experiences over the years, creating a tapestry of memories.

---

5 Kellogg Company, "Share Your Breakfast," accessed December 29, 2015, http://www.kelloggs.com/en_US/share-your-breakfast.html.

For example, one long-time employee posted his favorite Southwest photos from the early 1970s.[6]

This is not marketing; it's advocacy. These brand advocates are now sharing their passion about the brand and influencing their social media circles. The people they're influencing are making their buying decisions based upon what they think about a brand instead of buying because of information directed to them in an ad, which is also marketing.

A NEW DAY FOR ADVOCACY

Advocacy today is about solving issues and affecting change. It's a new day for advocacy; we've moved beyond "pass a bill; kill a bill." Now advocacy is about highlighting issues and supporting causes; it's integrating advocacy tactics with marketing strategies designed to influence decision makers and to change local, state, and federal policy and practice. That's the differentiator.

Advocacy is about uniting around common beliefs. It's about standing together and speaking publicly on an issue and letting the public know why forces are joining together.

NOW TRENDING

MCG has been tracking and implementing advocacy efforts for more than two decades. We've seen how advocacy is implemented across numerous industry sectors. With this data, we've been able to identify trends and best practices.

---

6 Southwest Airlines, "Nuts about Southwest," accessed February 25, 2016, https://blogsouthwest.com/blogsw/.

Here are three overarching trends that are having a great impact on advocacy success today, demonstrating why advocacy is so attractive for organizations to implement.

1. *The impact of social media.* The first of these global trends is the impact of social media, which is a revolution in the way stakeholders engage that is completely changing the landscape. Where advocacy, in the past, involved identifying the problem—the individual or group—and using time-consuming traditional channels to discuss a message, organize and activate advocates, and then evaluate results, social media makes these components of an advocacy campaign essentially instantaneous. We have the ability to engage large numbers of organizations and people in a dialogue and to track and measure our results. With technology, advocacy can be done faster and more effectively than ever before, and we can do it 24/7.

   Traditionally, if people were trying to engage others in a conversation, they would send out a news release. They may have called people to come to a meeting or a town hall session. Now, most of that communication can be done through social media channels. Instead of bringing two hundred people together in a physical setting, they're able to touch two million people through social media channels. The same message may be there, but the ability to reach people, get them engaged, and have their voice and perspective shared is now unprecedented. Engagement in advocacy activity is being taken to a whole new, efficient, and cost-effective level with social media.

2.   *The business strategy.* The second trend is that advocacy has become an embedded and integral component of overall business strategy. This means a more focused and strategic approach in how we engage in all communications strategies including marketing, public relations, public affairs, and regulatory affairs. These activities are all being looked at through a different lens—an advocacy lens—as they never were in the past.

Part of what we're seeing is the impact of third-party thought leaders on the business strategy. Especially in corporate America, there's a growing recognition that a company can have third-party champions who are out there talking about their products and services, becoming advocates and influencing their social circles to engage in activities that are even outside traditional sales and marketing.

A great example of this is TOMS. Ultimately, the company wants to sell products, but it's also put together a program whereby, for every pair of shoes, purse, or sunglasses purchased, one is given away to a child in need.[7] This advocacy creates a two-way conversation. TOMS is actually involved in community projects that have nothing to do with selling products, but the company is seeing third-party champions are helping to take its business to the next level, and the company consistently leverages that activity and incorporates those opportunities into its overall business strategy.

---

7 TOMS, accessed December 29, 2015, http://www.toms.com/.

In fact, corporate social responsibility (CSR) is an important driving factor in purchase decisions and brand consideration of audiences, especially millennials.

3.   *Nontraditional partners.* The third trend that we're seeing is nontraditional partners coming together. We're seeing public-private partnerships between diverse stakeholders who may have proprietary issues but who also see a more overarching goal that can be accomplished by partnering with other like-minded individuals or groups. Advocacy is bringing about significant results for organizations that have diverse stakeholders who are all voicing the same message—one that reinforces an overarching goal.

The pharmaceutical industry and patient advocacy groups often times have different goals. But today those two diverse groups occasionally come together to address larger and broader issues such as obesity or clinical trials. Another example of nontraditional groups coming together is in the mental health community and law enforcement. These two nontraditional partners are working together to address the conversations and public-policy issues surrounding awareness and treatment of people with mental illnesses during interactions with law enforcement.[8] Partnerships such as these demonstrate how advocacy today is very much about building capacity and visibility.

---

8 National Alliance on Mental Illness (NAMI), *State Mental Health Legislation 2015*: Trends, Themes and Effective Practices, December 2015, http://www.nami.org/About-NAMI/Publications-Reports/Public-Policy-Reports/State-Mental-Health-Legislation-2015/NAMI-StateMentalHealthLegislation2015.pdf.

In my twenty-four years of experience in developing advocacy campaigns and working with organizations ranging from not-for-profits to Fortune 500 companies, I've seen emerging trends that are shaping today's advocacy landscape. What started as a grassroots tool used by organizations to have an impact on policies has trickled into corporate America as consumers started to demand more societal impact or awareness from brands.

Woven throughout this book, I will address what I've come to recognize as two types of advocacy:

1. *Issues-based advocacy.* Advocacy in which organizations, individually or unified as a coalition of groups with similar goals, work to advance a particular policy, goal, or outcome. Examples could include passing a city noise ordinance; state or federal legislation to protect funding for services for a vulnerable population, such as the elderly or children; coming together to address substantive policy changes.

2. *Corporate advocacy.* One of the most remarkable outcomes of traditional advocacy is that passionate loyalists that come forward to unify their voices and share their stories. Corporate America has taken note of the effectiveness of these issue proponents. We've seen a shift where companies are beginning to create and communicate internal and external advocacy programs in order to develop their own brand ambassadors and product loyalists. The interesting thing about corporate advocacy is that a part of it comes at the demand of the consumer. Today's savvy consumers are buying products

and services from companies whose corporate social-responsibility programs align with their own beliefs and values. For example, companies give back to the communities in which they are located.

And the really cool outcome? The union of issues-based advocacy and corporate advocacy. In this book, you'll read about the importance of having a diverse group of stakeholders at the table. Decision makers take notice when organizations that may not have much in common rally around an issue or work in collaboration to advance a similar goal.

Whether you run a small not-for-profit organization or are the CEO of a corporation, this book will help you understand how advocacy can be an effective strategy to add to your toolbox and help you prepare an advocacy plan that moves your target audiences into meaningful action.

THREE KEYS TO UNLOCK YOUR ADVOCACY SUCCESS

- What problem are you trying to solve?
- Who will be most affected?
- How would your organization benefit from an advocacy effort?

CHAPTER 2

BUILDING THE FRAMEWORK

It is not the beauty of a building you should look at; it's the construction of the foundation that will stand the test of time.
—David Allen Coe

Regardless of the cause or issue, an advocacy campaign is no easy task. Sometimes, in spite of the best intentions, efforts fail because organizations don't leverage opportunities for advocacy to the greatest potential.

What's needed is a plan, a foundation. In this chapter, we'll discuss the framework for that plan.

Advocacy is about bringing diverse sets of stakeholders together and being very clear about the message and steps that need to be taken to resolve the ultimate issue. And that message must be continually repeated throughout your campaign.

The key to success is to build the foundation of your advocacy campaign before it begins. Often, there are natural third-party advocates who are willing to come together to talk about the value, features, and benefits of a product or service, but you've got to engage them from the start all the way to the end of your campaign.

Designing an advocacy effort begins with the framework. Begin by being very clear about the goals and objectives, the use of tactics, and identifying your advocates. You must also identify the opposition and determine how to best counter their message.

TEN-POINT ADVOCACY PLAN

Too often, organizations think that an advocacy plan must be thirty or forty pages long. It doesn't have to be lengthy to be powerful. And it doesn't have to be complicated, but it must have structure.

Your advocacy plan needs to be strategic; it must be well thought out, and ultimately, it must be well executed.

Here are ten components you should think through as you're writing and crafting an advocacy plan. This template will help answer key questions as you create a plan.

1. **Goals and objectives**
   - What is the challenge or opportunity you want to address?
   - What are the specific desired outcomes?
   - What is the approach to the effort? Is it local, state, national, or international?

2.   **Research**

- Who is the opposition?

- What is the opposition saying and through what vehicles?

- What are the facts surrounding the issue?

- What professional papers, journals, studies, or data can you reference to support your desired outcome?

- What has been or is currently being communicated through traditional or nontraditional media about the issue or problem?

- Who are the influential groups or individuals who should collaborate or who are already discussing the issue?

- Do you have the resources and capacity to implement the advocacy effort?

3.   **Target audience identification**

- Who are the target audiences you are trying to reach and move to action?

- Who are the internal champions who will conduct your advocacy effort?

- Who are the external champions who will conduct your advocacy effort?

4.   **Brand development**

- Have you established the brand for the effort (mission, vision, name, logo, tagline, etc.)?

- What are your messages to be communicated to each of the target audiences? Are those messages clear, concise, and memorable?

5. **Strategy**

   - Is the effort accomplished through a grassroots (broad base) and/or grasstops (specific key influencers) engagement?
   - Will the effort utilize new technology resources to reach target audiences?
   - What are the overarching actions needed to reach the goals?

6. **Tactics**

   - What specific communications activities will you implement? Will you utilize multiple channels such as media relations, social media, digital, or others?
   - Who is the most appropriate messenger(s) for each of the engagement activities?
   - Have you educated your advocates on the message and activities?
   - Have you meida trained your spokesperson(s)?

7. **Tool development**

   - What communication tools are needed for each strategy?
   - Have the tools been created for customization and distribution?

8. **Timeline**

   - What are important dates, events, or meetings that would impact the effort?
   - Are the activities timed appropriately to have the impact to accomplish the goal?

- Have you created a timeline to determine when each of the specific activities is being conducted?

9. **Budget**

   - What are the costs associated with the advocacy effort?
   - Has someone been identified to manage the budget?

10. **Measurement**

    - Have you set quantifiable ways to measure the success?
    - What process do you have in place to communicate the status of the advocacy effort?
    - Did you achieve the campaign goals?

Remember: Without a plan, your efforts are more than likely to fail. By using this template, regardless of your organization, industry, or goals, you'll be able to build a framework to begin your advocacy efforts.

THREE KEYS TO UNLOCK YOUR ADVOCACY SUCCESS

- What does success look like?
- Who are the right players to help execute the plan?
- Do you have a system to measure and quantify success?

CHAPTER 3

THE KEYS TO BRANDING

*In order to carry a positive action, we must
develop here a positive vision.*
—Dalai Lama

J ust as in marketing, branding is essential to any advocacy campaign because branding helps people connect with your efforts. The key to success in branding any advocacy engagement is to differentiate yourself. Let me demonstrate.

Close your eyes for a moment and imagine a row of ten apples in front of you. In this row there are nine bright red apples and one green apple. If you were to open your eyes and see the row of apples, your eye would automatically go to the green apple. Why is this?

We're hardwired to notice what's different.

So, be different when it comes to advocacy branding. Stand out.

Take, for example, the craze in 2011 of many organizations trumpeting their "green" advocacy initiatives. "Green" logos and labels were a major focus and popped up on everything from potato chips to automobiles. Today we know that being "green" is just one piece of being sustainable. The word suffers from overuse and, in some cases, misuse. "Green" no longer means what it used to and is, in fact, a brand non-differentiator. Organizations had to quickly learn that addressing the *issues* of sustainability were what would, in fact, separate them from the competition. Consumers want products that aren't just greener but are also better and offer some kind of personal benefit. Since the green craze, organizations have made their brand positioning much more sustainable by meshing green marketing into their corporate social responsibility plans to benefit the greater good.

The Green Effect initiative is a textbook example of how a company did sustainability right from an advocacy-branding initiative.[9] In 2009, SunChips joined with National Geographic to launch the Green Effect, which invited US consumers to come up with the best Earth-saving idea. The ideas were collected, and the top ten were posted on the Green Effect website. Members of the public were then invited to vote for their favorite. One winner was chosen by popular vote, and four others were chosen by a panel of judges. The winners each received $20,000 to put their ideas into action. From a branding standpoint, the idea was a success because it brought sustainability to the forefront in a way that was collaborative and that engaged audience (consumer) participation.

---

9 PR Newswire, "Frito-Lay's SunChips Brand and National Geographic Join Forces to Launch the 'Green Effect,'" news release, April 21, 2009, http://www.prnewswire.com/news-releases/frito-lays-sunchips-brand-and-national-geographic-join-forces-to-launch-the-green-effect-61879527.html.

A FEW MYTHS

Before we dive into developing the branding foundation for an advocacy initiative, let's start with dispelling a few myths about branding.

1. A brand is not a logo.

2. A brand is not an identity.

3. A brand is not a product.

So what exactly is a brand? A brand is a person's gut feeling about a product, service, or organization. Think about that for a second: *a brand is a gut feeling*.

Why is that? A brand is not what you say it is or what your company says it is. A brand is what your *target audience* says it is.

Knowing what consumers want from your brand is critical—even with an advocacy initiative. The next step is to gain traction with your brand in the marketplace.

Whether you are a Fortune 500 that is engaging in advocacy efforts to promote your sustainable products or a nonprofit that is fighting for health care access, there are key essentials of branding. You can't have a successful advocacy engagement without strong consideration of the brand.

ESSENTIAL #1: DIFFERENTIATE

As humans, we are programmed with a mental filter to help sift through the clutter. To be successful, your brand has to break through that filter. We live in a crowded marketplace of information and messages.

The most important thing you can do to differentiate your advocacy initiative is focus. Ask yourself the following:

- Why does it matter? This should be the emotional response to why your advocacy initiative exists.

- How do you do what you do? This should be your value proposition. It's where you highlight how you are different from your competition/opposition. In essence, this is the value of your advocacy endeavor, which, at its core, is an effort to create positive change.

- What do you do? This could be your products, services, or issues you support. What can be expected from the advocacy initiative?

ESSENTIAL #2: COLLABORATE

Building an advocacy brand is a collaborative project. Rome wasn't built in a day, and it wasn't built by one person; your brand won't be either.

It is important to engage key stakeholders or ambassadors to help shape the direction of your brand. Identify thought leaders and influencers within your industry who can bring insight to help you differentiate. Keep in mind that many of these key influencers may be right under your nose: your employees. As they interact with audiences on a daily basis, look for opportunities in which those key stakeholders can bring a unique knowledge to your organization and your advocacy initiative.

The SunChips partnership with National Geographic was a great example of a co-branded collaboration to expand the reach of an initiative. It enabled both organizations to reach a broader group of individuals with the message of sustainability, encouraging people to take part in doing good at the local level.

ESSENTIAL #3: INNOVATE

Innovation through creativity is critical to giving your brand more exposure in the marketplace. Creativity, used in strategic ways, can help you accomplish this.

Take, for example, the National Breast Cancer Coalition with its cutting-edge creativity and excellence demonstrated at each touch point of its advocacy campaign, the Breast Cancer Deadline 2020.[10] The organization proclaims this is a movement to end breast cancer by the close of the decade because, the organization says, advocates need something more than hope. Hope is a wish. The deadline is a commitment.

How can you tell when an idea is innovative? When it scares the hell out of everybody. Now, I use "everybody" loosely because you have to think back to the boardroom meeting when this concept was discussed. I imagine some executives voiced bold concerns about their ability to make the commitment. But innovation should be bold—and at times a little scary. That's how we see true change in our world.

---

10 National Breast Cancer Coalition, "Are You with Us?", accessed December 29, 2015, www.breast-cancerdeadline2020.org.

ESSENTIAL #4: VALIDATE

Validation means bringing the audience into the creative process. The old communication model was a monologue. A sender has a message, and it's communicated to the receiver. The new communication model is a dialogue. The emphasis is on the receiver communicating back to the sender. This model is more of a continuous circle.

The question here is whether you, as a leader, are listening to what your audiences have to say.

The old communication model was a monologue:

SENDER ▶ MESSAGE ▶ RECEIVER

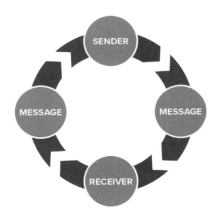

The new communication model is a dialogue:

The emphasis is on the receiver communicating back to the sender.

Are you listening to what your audiences have to say?

ESSENTIAL #5: CULTIVATE

A brand is a living concept and should be constantly evolving and nurtured over time.

Think about Starbucks. Starbucks has developed a brand that is so much more than coffee. Starbucks demonstrates a persona that extends beyond its brand's functional benefits. This is demonstrated through the company's service interactions, packaging, décor, product offerings, corporate culture, and advocacy initiatives. The bottom line is that Starbucks cultivates a brand character that showcases its personality and the relationship with its audience.

The five essentials of branding can serve to anchor and evolve your brand, but if you really want to connect with consumers, you'll also do the following:

- *Help your audience achieve its goals.* Nine out of ten individuals want organizations to help them reach their personal goals, and they want to be asked what they need to attain them, not be told how to do so.[11] These personal goals can, oftentimes, align with advocacy initiatives that do good in the world.

- *Listen and respond thoughtfully.* Forty percent of consumers want organizations to pay better attention to what they're saying and demonstrate this through thoughtful response.[12]

---

11 Edelman, "It Pays to Share," Brandshare Global Results, accessed November 12, 2015, http://www.edelman.com/insights/intellectual-property/brandshare/about-brandshare/downloads/.
12 Ibid.

- *Be transparent and honest in all that you do. Fast Company* says only 3 percent of consumers actually believe businesses are honest and transparent.[13] Be up front about your advocacy alignment, the *why* of supporting or directly engaging in advocacy campaigns.

- *Align your values with those of your target market.* An overwhelming number of people want to do business with organizations that share their beliefs.

- *Share experiences, but make them about people.* Eighty-two percent of consumers want companies to share experiences focused on real people.

It's important to remember that your advocacy initiatives are not always achieved in one year; they're often multi-year efforts. So your brand should never be static. It must evolve and adapt to the changing environment, but it must also continue to maintain its core essence as it heads toward its goal. And as you continually evolve your brand, you must also continue to educate your internal and external audiences. If you truly want to give your consumers what they want, you'll listen to, and involve them in, your company's story as it continues to unfold and as your brand is elevated.

KEY ELEMENTS OF A BRAND FOR YOUR ADVOCACY PROGRAM

Now that we've established that a brand is not what *you* say it is but rather what *they* say it is, it's time to start building your brand.

---

13 Ibid.

When you launch an advocacy campaign, the brand must be there for people to rally around. It must be strong and compelling. If the brand is diluted, your competition will run over you.

At MCG, we've worked with hundreds of companies, large and small, to help develop their advocacy brands or enhance brand traction in the marketplace. If there's one thing we've learned, it's that branding is personal—to you and to your target audiences.

Here are seven key must-haves to use in creating your own advocacy brand.

1. *Name.* The way you name and frame your advocacy campaign often emerges from the facts you choose to highlight within your issue. How you present your issue has everything to do with how well it will "sell" in the marketplace of ideas.

   A strong name must not be tied to a passing trend, hard to pronounce, or difficult to remember. It must have the ability to grow with your organization, be available and protectable, convey positive connotations, and lend itself to visual representation.[14] For an advocacy campaign, most names are descriptive, but do not have to be, as a rule.

2. *Tagline.* A tagline captures the essence of an advocacy campaign's personality in a concise phrase.[15] Taglines require consistent use and, essentially, become shorthand for what a brand stands for and delivers. While a variety of criteria are used to create a powerful tagline, the following provide a quick snapshot:

---

14 Alina Wheeler, *Designing Brand Identity* (New Jersey: John Wiley & Sons, Inc., 2013), 22-23.
15 Alina Wheeler, *Designing Brand Identity*, 24-25.

- short (seven words or less)

- different from competitors

- easy to say and remember

- no negative connotation

- looks good in a small font

- can be protected and trademarked

- evokes an emotional response

3. *Messaging/voice.* Brand messages should distill the essence of the advocacy initiative and grow with repetition to differentiate the brand. They should be brief, clear, and precise. It's also important to determine your tone of voice—essentially, how your brand says what it says. The best brands speak with one distinctive voice, regardless of the platform or target audience.[16] Think about the brands that are so clear in their voice that you can almost hear their key messages when you say their name. As an example, what words would you use to describe the voice you hear when you think of Walt Disney World? You may say it's fun, clever, and imaginative. How about for the Boy Scouts? Perhaps it's trustworthy, adventurous, patriotic, and faithful.

4. *Logo.* A logo is a powerful vessel to help people understand what your advocacy campaign stands for since logos are the most frequent brand reminder. As a company's major graphical representation, a logo anchors a brand and becomes the single most-visible manifestation of the company within the target market.

---

16 Alina Wheeler, *Designing Brand Identity*, 26-27.

For this reason, a well-designed logo is an essential part of any marketing strategy.

The best logos stand for something—they have a meaning and a backstory, whether it's a big idea or a brand promise. In 2010, The University of Texas MD Anderson Cancer Center updated its logo with a graphical element that scratched through the word "cancer" with a red line and immediately told you its mission: to eradicate cancer. The intent of the mark was to make clear to all those who touch MD Anderson the commitment to its mission and optimism on making this happen.[17]

5. *Color palette.* Color is used to express personality and evoke emotion. Using colors in a consistent manner reinforces brand integrity. [18] For example, if you see a small gift box in a distinct robin's-egg blue, you immediately know it's from Tiffany & Co. Likewise, you pick up a red cola can, feeling confident it is a Coca-Cola. Individual colors have meaning, and together, a color palette can symbolize the brand's promise. For example, Feeding America's color palette utilizes orange (the color of hunger) and green (signifying rebirth, regeneration, and growth). However, beyond the psychology behind them, colors should also be tested for effectiveness. Once you've selected the colors that best represent your brand and advocacy initiative, stick to them for consistency.

17 "New MD Anderson Logo Challenges Employees, Public to Aspire to a World Without Cancer." MD Anderson Cancer Center, accessed February 29, 2016. https://www.mdanderson.org/news-room/2010/05/new-logo---aspires-for-world-without-cancer.html.
18 Alina Wheeler, *Designing Brand Identity*, 150-151.

6. *Imagery.* Photography, graphics, and illustrations play an important role in the look and feel of a brand. We live in a visually rich world, and we naturally gravitate toward genuine, authentic visuals, whether on social media, advertisements, or websites. Photography can make or break the success of branding an advocacy campaign, yet it's often the last consideration in the brand-development process. While high-end stock photography can do the trick, consider capturing original photography. Complementary graphics, infographics, and illustrations can also provide strong visual support.

7. *Brand guidelines.* Brand guidelines are needed to manage the consistency and integrity of a brand-identity system.[19] The guidelines should be easily accessible to internal and external audiences who will be communicating about, and representing, your brand. Maintaining a brand is a shared responsibility of every employee, partner, and advocate. Sticking to the guidelines will save money, time, and frustration while building the brand. Brand guidelines help users implement the brand's visual identity easily and accurately by outlining logo usage, color palette, typography, printing recommendations, image direction, and example executions.

Armed with these brand elements, your organization will be ready to stand out with its advocacy initiative. It's also important to remember that brands, even for advocacy, are built over time. Your brand will continuously evolve as you foster its growth.

---

19 Alina Wheeler, *Designing Brand Identity*, 202-203.

By setting your sights on the horizon, keeping track of market trends, staying on top of the needs of your customers or advocates, and following the tips in this chapter, you'll be poised to take advantage of opportunities to grow your brand to become increasingly relevant to your target audience and to your advocacy efforts.

THREE KEYS TO UNLOCK YOUR ADVOCACY SUCCESS

- How does your advocacy campaign brand differentiate you?

- Is your brand known so advocates can speak with passion and conviction?

- Does your brand message have awareness and call-to-action elements?

CHAPTER 4

A FOCUS ON INTERNAL AUDIENCES

Individual commitment to a group effort—that is what makes a team work, a company work, a society work, a civilization work.
—Vince Lombardi

Your internal communications program is a foundational component for successful advocacy efforts. Remember, you're likely to find many of your best advocates right in your own backyard. Internal audiences are your employees, board members, and funders—the individuals or groups within (or closely associated with) your organization. These internal audiences are key to the success of any advocacy campaign, and you need them with you from the beginning of your program. Another aspect of advocacy is corporate social responsibility (CSR)—programs focused on promoting social change. This type of corporate citizenship has the opportunity to strengthen your relationship with internal and external advocates.

We've identified several reasons why engaging internal audiences in your advocacy initiative is essential. Internal audiences:

- increase awareness of the organization and its brand and/ or advocacy initiative

- improve brand position in the marketplace and in the minds and hearts of audiences

- make it easier for all audiences—whether policymakers, customers, or board members—to find answers to their questions

- improve the organization's ability to hire the best talent and recruit the best volunteers

- decrease the costs of engaging external audiences by being recognized as thought leaders

Organizations often use their internal audiences in marketing products and services, but you can do the same when looking to affect issues, change policy, and drive corporate social responsibility. Employees are too often an untapped resource, yet they can be some of those boots on the ground to help you in your advocacy efforts.

What your employees think, say, and do has a significant impact on your success. By turning employees into trusted communication ambassadors, companies bring their strongest asset and their most vocal internal advocates in direct contact with their customer base— their external target audiences. In order to have an effective advocacy campaign, you must create a unified effort by educating, empowering, and exciting your champions. You must do this from the start of your campaign, and it must be a deliberate effort.

Employee advocacy is a measurable approach to growing your reach through word of mouth—the rawest, yet strongest, form of any type of promotion. Employees can be the proudest, loudest, and most knowledgeable ambassadors a company has, particularly when it comes to the benefits of products and services their company delivers or in vocalizing the impact an issue is going to have on them, their families, their friends, and their communities. Employees bring a unique combination of expertise, authenticity, and close communications to an organizational initiative that is unmatched by even the best-run external-advocate program. They can be the face of the issue for which you are trying to advocate and your strongest, most effective and efficient resource to, ultimately, achieve your advocacy effort.

A great example of employees-as-internal-ambassadors was achieved by Starbucks. In February 2008 the company closed down every single store on one day.[20] Its 7,100 stores were closed for three hours to conduct training for partners (as the company calls its employees). The event was, according to a news release, part of the company's ongoing efforts to "renew its focus on the customer."

Closing the stores was a potent form of internal communication. This act sent an unmistakable message that the company's iconic founder, Howard Schultz, was serious about his expectations

---

20 Michelle Kung, "Starbucks Closing Stores Today," The Huffington Post, accessed February 29, 2016, http://www.huffingtonpost.com/2008/02/25/starbucks-closing-stores-_n_88447.html.

that all 135,000 Starbucks employees deliver on the brand promise. Closing the stores was a bold move by Starbucks to take a step back, look at employees as the company's best ambassadors, and find ways to train them further to do their jobs even better.

Internal communication is simply having a continuous process in place to ensure your employees understand the *why* and *who* behind your business proposition. Oftentimes, for organizations, internal communication is the missing link between perception and reality, promise and delivery, effective marketing and positive outcomes.

Most companies will expend a great deal of effort on their external marketing. But what if all of the brilliant insights gained in the external communications process could be ingrained in the mind of each employee? What if there were a deliberate step in the process to help employees not only perform their functions better but also more intimately understand those whom they serve? What if each and every employee could be enabled and equipped to be a powerful steward of the organization and its advocacy initiatives?

Each year, Gallup issues a report on employee engagement. The 2015 report showed employee engagement at 31.5 percent, the highest level since the organization first began measuring performance in 2000.[21] Engagement began to drop in 2008 during the financial collapse and continued to fall in 2009. It did not show any signs of improvement until 2011, and it reached its current peak in 2014.[22] Organizations are starting to take notice of employee engagement in a bigger way. And there's still a tremendous amount of opportunity for companies to engage in internal advocacy.

---

21 Amy Adkins, "U.S. Employee Engagement Steady in September, at 32%," October 16, 2015, accessed December 29, 2015, http://www.gallup.com/poll/186212/employee-engagement-steady-september.aspx?g_source=EMPLOYEE_ENGAGEMENT&g_medium=topic&g_campaign=tiles.
22 Adkins, Amy, "Majority of U.S. Employees Not Engaged Despite Gains in 2014." Gallup.com. Accessed February 29, 2016. http://www.gallup.com/poll/181289/majority-employees-not-engaged-despite-gains-2014.aspx.

CULTIVATING COMMUNICATION AMBASSADORS

To begin cultivating internal-communication ambassadors, start by looking at your organizational culture. Look at your core values: who you are, what you do, and what you stand for. Then cultivate this for your employees and other internal audiences.

Here are some suggestions for getting started:

- *Encourage employee social media interaction for your advocacy initiative.* We'll discuss the power of social media in depth in a later chapter.

- *Allow employees to help strengthen relationships among all target audiences.* Create a sense of shared ownership in the goals of the organization, and focus on using employee experience and feedback to improve products/services and customer service. For example, if our goal is to find a cure for cancer, would we be more focused on getting a health care bill passed or obtaining funding for research?

- *Create channels of communication.* Look at ways to create internal forms of communication to aid your internal audience in their efforts. In working with companies small or large on both internal and external advocacy programs, we've found that communication with advocates is not only vital but profitable, as they are invested in improving the products/services and spreading the word of mouth around your brand. They want to be heard, they want to have a relationship with your company. You need an easy way for both your internal and external advocates to offer suggestions, and they need to feel their suggestions are acknowledged and considered.

- *Invest in employee well-being.* A little goes a long way when it comes to showing your employees they're appreciated. When you invest in employees as internal stakeholders in a bigger way, they will be more willing to be brand champions.

- *Make sharing easy for your internal advocates.* Organizations should make it as easy as possible for employees to share their brand experience. Opportunities may include adding "share" buttons to websites, supplying employees with messaging and graphics for communications campaigns, and allowing them to be actively involved as the "faces" of the company.

CORPORATE SOCIAL RESPONSIBILITY

Corporate social responsibility (CSR) is another concept that is ingrained in advocacy and, as I mentioned earlier, is often driven by employees. CSR is a management concept whereby companies integrate social and environmental concerns in their business operations and interactions with their stakeholders.

It's interesting to note that not too long ago, a business's consumers, shareholders, and employees were most concerned with price, profits, or paychecks, known as the three Ps. But today, that just doesn't cut it. Modern stakeholders expect companies to go above and beyond to contribute to the greater good. According to a survey conducted by *Forbes*, 88 percent of consumers think that alongside achieving their business goals, companies should also work to improve society and the environment.[23]

In their most basic form, CSR programs devote companies' time, money, and support to social, environmental, or economic welfare efforts. And the goal is not to add funds to the corporate coffers but rather to foster positive change in the world and the communities where these companies are located. This, in itself, is advocacy making positive change in the world.

When CSR is done well, however, not only will a company bring about meaningful change outside its walls; it will also reap other benefits.

The efforts that are best for your organization are typically programs that make the most sense for your business, its personality, and its purpose. At Moore Communications Group, we let the individual passions of our employees drive the outreach we do through MCG Impact, our established community outreach program. Since 2010, we have had the opportunity to work with more than thirty-five nonprofits in a variety of ways, including providing organizations with communications support, feeding the less fortunate, hosting a day of activities for seniors, sending letters to veterans, and so much more. CSR has become part of MCG's culture.

---

23 James Epstein-Reeves, "Consumers Overwhelmingly Want CSR," *Forbes,* December 15, 2010, accessed November 12, 2015, http://www.forbes.com/sites/csr/2010/12/15/new-study-consumers-demand-companies-implement-csr-programs/.

YOUR ADVOCACY GOODWILL WILL BE REWARDED

Companies that support the greater good enjoy a variety of benefits, just a few of which include:

- earning a reputation as a company that cares

- gaining brand recognition

- promoting the organization's brand in a positive light

- strengthening the business's ties to the communities in which it operates

- boosting employee morale and attracting more qualified applicants

- generating more media attention and good public relations

- seeing increases in revenue—customers want to do business with companies that help their community to make the world a better place

While it takes a bit of time to realize these benefits, a strong social responsibility policy is well worth the energy and expense. Having a strong and trustworthy reputation is invaluable, and consumer, media, and employee appreciation will naturally follow.

CSR is the key to winning consumers while advocating and creating change in issues that impact our communities and our world. It is becoming more mainstream as forward-thinking companies embed caring into the core of their business operations to create shared value for business and society. This form of advocacy has become vital for business success.

THREE KEYS TO UNLOCK YOUR ADVOCACY SUCCESS

🔑 How effective are your internal branding efforts?

🔑 What internal audiences could be ambassadors for change?

🔑 Do you have a dedicated CSR program to amplify your advocacy engagement?

CHAPTER 5

CREATING AND MOBILIZING CHAMPIONS

No one can whistle a symphony; it takes a whole orchestra to play it.
—Halford E. Luccock

This quote is used in many team-building exercises and is attributed to Halford E. Luccock (1885–1961), a professor of homiletics at Yale Divinity School. The story goes that Professor Luccock gave this reply when he was told that Miss Daisy Brown could whistle Beethoven's *Fifth Symphony*. As the professor implies, obviously one person cannot create the volume, complexity, or intensity that is required of a symphony by whistling solo. You need many different instruments to join together to make it come alive.[24]

Advocacy is about making a core group of passionate champions' voices come alive to have a positive impact on issues or concerns that affect people and their communities.

So how do you identify champions for your issue? Always begin with a base. Find those individuals or organizations that understand the issue, are already talking about the issue, and are willing to publicly step out and join you with their voices and resources. You can identify them by doing some research.

A key area of advocacy research is stakeholder mapping. Through this process, we assess individuals and organizations in the identified industry areas, provide insight into their reach and influence, and highlight opportunities and challenges for engagement. This allows us to assist organizations in prioritizing their resources to ensure strategic advocacy engagement and outreach.

Here are seven questions to help you identify and locate champions:

1. Who has been personally affected by your issue? This may be an individual activist, business colleagues, or an advocacy organization. You should create a database of these key potential supporters.

2. Who has spoken in support of your issue or similar issues in the past? You may want to align with this group or have it join yours.

---

24 The Big Apple, "'No one can whistle a symphony; it takes a whole orchestra to play it' (teamwork aphorism)," The Big Apple, accessed February 29, 2016, http://www.barrypopik.com/index.php/ new_york_city/entry/no_one_can_whistle_a_symphony_it_takes_a_whole_orchestra_to_play_it_ teamwor.

3.	Who is currently engaged in a conversation about your issue on social media platforms? What is their message? What tactics are they using? How effective is their reach?

4.	Is it more strategic to become part of an existing coalition than to create a new one? Weigh the advantages and disadvantages of supporting and engaging in an existing coalition with similar goals, objectives, and vision.

5.	Who would you like to collaborate with so that you are not going it alone? Will your advocacy campaign be more successful utilizing grassroots, grasstops, or both?

6.	Which potential collaborators have sufficient resources? You want to join with groups or organizations that bring assets to the table.

7.	Are there potential pitfalls in joining other coalitions regarding funding, policies, relationships, or past activities that may have a negative impact on your brand?

Once you have conducted your research, reaching out and starting a conversation may lead to collaborative efforts. Recognize that you will need to have a clear and concise vision of what is to be accomplished and how joining the effort will lead to success.

IT TAKES A UNIFIED VOICE

In today's aggressive and sometimes negative atmosphere in the media and in politics, a single voice cannot rise above the noise and be heard. One of the greatest examples of a multivoice activation is Mothers Against Drunk Driving (MADD). MADD began with one outraged mother and expanded to become a group of extraordinary people banding together to help change the way society views and punishes drunk driving.[25] Before MADD, most people did not recognize drunk driving as a real problem in our country. Coalitions like MADD, including Remove Intoxicated Drivers (RID) and Students Against Destructive Decisions (SADD), have made a profound difference in efforts to change public perception and strengthen laws to address the problem of impaired driving. With more than two million members and brand recognition that is off the charts, what began as a small, committed group of advocates has grown into a movement and offshoots that are saving thousands of lives.

You need to identify and recruit individuals and organizations that naturally align with your cause. *The Merriam-Webster Dictionary* defines coalition as "the action or process of joining together with another or others for a common purpose."[26] Whether you call it a coalition, partnership, alliance, or network, it becomes a group that sees the benefit in working together with other advocates for a common goal. Although there may be challenges in building a coalition, a loud, unified voice is a great asset.

Passionate volunteers with a loud, unified voice brought about change addressing the disparity in cancer treatment options. The Alliance for Access to Cancer Care[27] was a Florida coalition Moore Communications Group created in 2013. The coalition—composed of thousands of supporters reflecting the interests of patients, physicians, caregivers, health care organizations, the business community, and elected officials—joined together to tell the story about disparity

25 MADD, "The History of MADD," accessed December 29, 2015, http://www.madd.org/about-us/history/.
26 *The Merriam-Webster Dictionary*, "Coalition," accessed December 29, 2015, http://www.merriam-webster.com/dictionary/coalition.
27 "Proposed Legislation Would Give Cancer Patients Improved Access to Life-Saving Treatments Prescribed by Physicians," Jeff Atwater Florida's Chief Financial Officer, accessed February 29, 2016, http://www.myfloridacfo.com/sitePages/newsroom/pressRelease.aspx?id=4133.

in patients' costs of cancer treatment. The issue was that treatments provided intravenously were covered under a health plan's medical benefit, with only a co-pay required from the patient. But orally administered cancer treatments were covered under the insurer's pharmacy benefit, which resulted in high out-of-pocket patient costs.[28] This alliance of diverse advocate champions raised awareness of the problem, proposed a solution, and brought about an effective change in the state, becoming an example for state policy throughout the US. As of October 2015, forty states have enacted oral-chemotherapy laws.[29]

In the past twenty-four years, our firm has built coalitions within individual states and across the country, representing hundreds of thousands of individuals and bringing together varied organizations as virtual networks to work for a common cause. These coalitions reflect interests in a variety of industry sectors: health care, environment, workforce, finance, telecommunications, education, and others. What is common among these coalitions is a desire to see change take place and the commitment to stand together to accomplish that change.

Another recent example of uniting like-minded groups to create change was a grassroots coalition created by Moore Communication Group to address the issue of staged automobile accidents and questionable insurance claims. This diverse coalition, composed of business owners, consumer advocates, and law-enforcement officials, was branded "Put the Brakes on Accident Fraud."[30] The coalition's mission was to serve as the amplified voice urging legis-

---

28 Ibid.

29 Patients Equal Access Coalition (PEAC), "Oral Chemotherapy Access Legislative Landscape, October 2015, http://peac.myeloma.org/oral-chemo-access-map/.

30 "Put the Brakes on Accident Fraud," news release, February 24, 2012, http://static-lobbytools. s3.amazonaws.com/press/45141_onomic_affairs_committee_for_advancing_pip_fraud_legislation. pdf.

lators to rise above special-interest pressures and pass true reform to reduce no-fault fraud and lower auto-insurance rates. From the very beginning, building a firm foundation allowed the participants to establish goals and priorities and map out strategies. Hundreds of coalition members participated in a variety of activities such as media outreach, special events, letter writing, social media efforts, and so on. Within three months, anti-fraud legislation was passed and signed into law by the governor.

ADVOCACY RESEARACH

In 2014–2015, MCG conducted a set of interviews of more than 120 C-suite-level professionals from more than one hundred state and national health care, nonprofit, and advocacy organizations, including those representing cardiovascular health, mental health, oncology, women's health, and aging. Three primary themes that emerged in the surveys were the need for capacity building, the need to better coordinate networks and coalitions, and their desire to be viewed as collaborative peers in public affairs activities.

CAPACITY BUILDING

As technology has advanced and individuals and organizations have more channels to express their thoughts on issues, the need to become more sophisticated in advocacy efforts has increased. Especially among nonprofit and start-up organizations, capacity building is a concern: How do organizations educate their internal and external stakeholders on messages, tactics, tools, and resources to accomplish their goals? Many advocacy groups are just trying to keep afloat financially, so dollars may not be available for professional development training for staff and volunteers. During the C-suite study, I heard pleas for help in strategic planning, board development, assessment of internal-communications vehicles, consensus building, social and digital media, public affairs efforts, and media training for leadership. This was especially true for local, state, and regional groups with fewer resources.

BETTER COORDINATION

A greater coordination of networks and coalitions is needed. The advocacy landscape has evolved dramatically, with more groups than ever forming to create change in their communities, the nation, and the world. This proliferation of advocacy groups means that to survive and accomplish your goals, you need to be strategic and focused while not duplicating the efforts of others.

Our research found that advocacy groups and champions want to become catalysts and facilitators for broader discussions on issues that relate to their own. Organizations seek opportunities to network and coordinate with groups for mutual success. The desire to coordinate facilitates greater engagement. For example, if the advocacy effort focuses its concerns on hunger in America, broader discussions with advocacy groups focused on poverty, access to healthy food, health care, affordable housing, and living wages would likely occur.

COLLABORATIVE PEERS

How coalitions are built has changed over time. Beginning in the 1980s through the first decade of the twenty-first century, many advocacy relationships were built on a model of a dominant group creating the brand, developing the messages, identifying the legislative channels, and then asking other groups to join it as additional champions amplifying its message. It was the old, "It's my ball, so play the game my way." As the executive director of a national advocacy organization once told me, "If you are the eight hundred-pound gorilla, then you get to make the decisions."

The alliance development model has now been redefined as organizations binding together and recognizing each other as collaborative peers. Each participating group within the coalition is seen as a unique and valuable partner. This model allows everyone involved to help set the vision and direction, establish overarching, consistent messages that can be tailored to their internal stakeholders and have engagement that fits resource bandwidth. It also means organizations that in the past might not have felt they could participate now have the sense they can have a seat at the decision making table.

An example of this alliance development model of peers is the national "I Am (Still) Essential" coalition.[31] Multiple organizations with specific missions joined together to bring attention to concerns surrounding 2014 silver insurance plans, which they believed reflected limited benefits, high-cost sharing, and lack of transparency and uniformity. Founding partners of this coalition, the AIDS Institute, National Alliance on Mental Illness (NAMI), and the Epilepsy Foundation recognized the unique strengths, relationships, and resources that each brought to the coalition; one interest did not try to dominate another.

Although three of the organizations may have been more active in setting the initial direction of the overall effort, as more and more joined the coalition, no individual group was made to feel insignificant or unwelcomed. According to the AIDS Institute's website,

---

31 Lisa Stand, "I Am (Still) Essential Coalition," The AIDS Institute, October 2, 2014, accessed December 30, 2015, http://www.theaidsinstitute.org/sites/default/files/attachments/L.%20Stand%20 I%20Am%20Still%20Essential%20Coalition.pdf.

in a letter to Secretary Sylvia Mathews Burwell (July 2014), more than 330 organizations—including the national and state chapters of organizations representing people with HIV/AIDS, epilepsy, hepatitis, mental health, lupus, kidney, leukemia, and lymphoma, just to name a few—noted, "These issues need attention if the ACA [Affordable Care Act] is to deliver on its promises for people with chronic health concerns."[32]

There is a recognized shift toward building long-term, mutually beneficial relationships based on aligned goals, respect, and transparency. For example, leaders in the pharmaceutical industry have worked hard to strengthen relationships with advocates and organizations to achieve a mutual trust level in which appropriate strategic partnerships and collaboration efforts are launched to jointly address public policy. Although there are issues on which the pharmaceutical industry and patient advocacy groups will never align, there are some natural fits such as the support for access to life-saving medications and innovation in research. It is this nexus of mutually aligned public affairs goals that makes working in this collaboration successful.

In this collaborative peer model, groups jointly identify, develop, recruit, and engage. The advantage is multifaceted: shared risk, cost savings, maximized resources, and accelerated solutions to concentrate on short-term and long-term solutions.

This new model and the desire to be "collaborative peers" having an equal partnership are reflected in the following coalition model.

---

32 The AIDS Institute, "I Am (Still) Essential," July 28, 2014, accessed December 30, 2015, http://www.theaidsinstitute.org/sites/default/files/attachments/IAmStillEssentialBurwellltr_0.pdf.

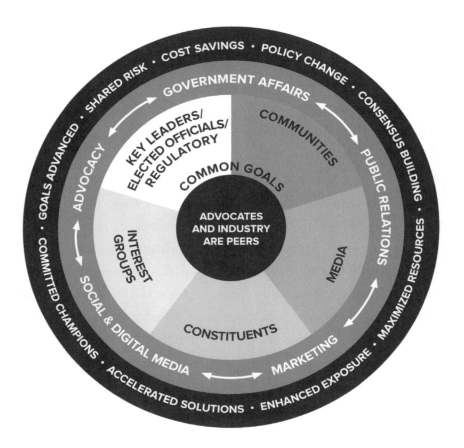

FOUR RECOMMENDATIONS FOR BUILDING ADVOCACY

Working with coalitions has allowed MCG to produce hundreds of award-winning alliance development campaigns. That experience has led us to form these four recommendations for any organizations looking to build an advocacy program:

1. Make sure that both quality and quantity of stakeholder participation are equally considered. Numbers are important, but if alignment does not make sense to you, it will not to others either.

2. In the relationship-building process, engage with potential allies earlier rather than later so they can participate in the development of the strategy, goals, and objectives. This will facilitate buy-in.

3. Focus on diversifying the base, bringing in nontraditional allies to strengthen the coalition. The broader and more diverse the participation, the more power and substance the coalition will reflect.

4. Identify a leader for the effort. As the saying goes, when trying to build a wooden horse, a committee without a leader will create a three-hump camel!

GRASSROOTS AND GRASSTOPS

In any advocacy effort, a decision needs to be made on whether to strategically engage in a grassroots or grasstops campaign, or both.

In a 2007 *Politico* article, Chris Frates, now at CNN, said, "The more familiar grassroots approach identifies a large group and urges them to blast decision makers with a message. These efforts are often publicized and aimed at demonstrating popular support for an issue. Grasstops, however, stealthily seek out influential local community leaders or personal friends, such as a chamber of commerce president or golfing buddy, to make the case directly."[33] I believe his explanation simply and clearly defines grassroots versus grasstops.

33 Chris Frates, "In Lobbying, Communication Goes Both Ways," Politico, June 28, 2007, accessed November 4, 2015, http://www.politico.com/story/2007/06/in-lobbying-communication-goes-both-ways-004703.

A well-orchestrated advocacy campaign employs both grassroots and grasstops simultaneously. Impact is made when mass communication by advocates, through channels such as letter writing, e-mails, tweets, and phone calls (grassroots), reinforces direct conversations by key opinion leaders (grasstops) with elected officials. Integrate into your efforts traditional public relations and media-relations activities and the aggressive uses of social media platforms, and you have a powerful engine to drive change.

For example, we were working on a piece of legislation and had coordinated a meeting with grassroots advocates and the chairman of the last committee assigned to the bill before moving to the floor. Due to unfortunate timing, the chairman only had three minutes to speak while en route to the committee meeting. Instead of sharing a spiral bound packet or facts and figures, we shared the story of "Gary" and the impact that this legislation would have on this man. In his haste, we didn't think the chairman retained Gary's story. We took our seats in the gallery of the committee room where the Chairman said, "Now committee members, let me tell you a story about my friend, Gary." The legislation passed unanimously. The story of one constituent is infinitely more powerful than anything else.

ORGANIZATIONAL MODELS

Just as there is no one-size-fits-all advocacy implementation plan, the same can be said for an internal advocacy structure. Organizations have to consider their priorities, capacity to execute a strategy, and overall goals and objectives. In this section, I'll share the organizational models I have coined to reflect the various structures used by my clients in regulated industries. The following are some options (or a hybrid combination of options) for how other industries think about and build their own internal advocacy structure.

1. *Spoke and wheel* is a centralized model. All advocacy efforts are coordinated from a centralized point within the organization or coalition. The model is streamlined and single-leadership driven. Its vision and goals are clearly communicated internally and externally with all collaborative peers. And its relationships and activities are managed from the spoke position radiating out to all stakeholders.

2. *Tic-tac-toe* is a moderately centralized model. The management of relationships and efforts are centralized but could be bifurcated, recognizing different focuses such as national versus state, national versus international, and so on. The model still has a centralized point within the organization or coalition, but it could have multiple leaders focusing on specific areas.

3. *Community of practice* reflects advocacy in an organization or coalition that has multiple efforts or advocacy in like-minded organizations that are affiliated and keep each other informed about activities and engagement but do not, officially, combine forces. There is no one single leader or point of administration. The organizations and individual leaders communicate on a regular basis but see each other more as occasional partners or valued colleagues in the overall advocacy sphere.

4. *Silo* refers to an organization or coalition that sees its effort as singly focused. The organization believes that there is little need for partnering or communicating with potential collaborative peers. The organization has a mission and believes it can achieve it without outside influencers. This model primarily exists within a large organization where colleagues and other like-minded individuals/organizations don't even know that an advocacy campaign is being undertaken.

Over the past decade or so, I have seen numerous organizations moving from very decentralized models to more centralized models. This tends to occur as an advocacy program becomes more mature, and leadership begins to recognize the value of building mutually beneficial relationships with third-party groups. But the trend at the moment is toward tic-tac-toe and community-of-practice models. This is due, in part, to mergers, corporate downsizing, and spreading the advocacy efforts and relationship management over a broader group of internal stakeholders to better support governmental affairs and broader corporate objectives.

There is no right or wrong model. Each should reflect the needs of the organization, its corporate objectives, and its resources. No matter your model, the commitment to identify champions and engage them is essential.

THREE KEYS TO UNLOCK YOUR ADVOCACY SUCCESS

What other organizations could be natural allies in your coalition?

Which type of campaign makes the most sense for your issue: grassroots and/or grasstops?

Which organizational model will work best with your efforts?

CHAPTER 6

INFLUENCING
PUBLIC POLICY

*Never measure the height of a mountain until you have
reached the top. Then you will see how low it was.*
—Dag Hammerskjold

T hroughout this book, we've been talking about the many
different forms of advocacy. As we've said, advocacy is
about having influence. When thinking about influence,
especially in public policy, coalitions and advocates need to take
into consideration certain factors before delivering their message to
elected officials.

Coalitions and champions of your issue that are ready to go out and take action need to know what to do before, during, and after interaction with policymakers—at the congressional level, the state legislature level, or with elected officials in public institutions—to have a more positive and long-term effect on public policy.

BE PREPARED

Before engaging with any elected officials, you really must prepare. You must familiarize yourself with policymakers' backgrounds. What is their voting record? What is their interest in your particular issue? How informed are they about your issue, and have they ever been engaged in something similar to your issue? That preparatory work is important. You want to be able to go into these conversations ready to succinctly address your key points. You also should be able to address, if appropriate, the arguments of your opponents.

In preparing for a conversation with an elected official, reflect on your purpose and be able to relate that purpose in an "elevator speech." Elected officials have a very limited amount of time, and frankly, they have limited attention spans because of so many priorities that are put on them. So what is your elevator speech? Does it clearly communicate the why, how, and what of the issue or program of concern to you and the elected official? Here's an example of an elevator speech we have developed for one of our clients:

Why: More than 3.5 million of our neighbors in Florida struggle to afford nutritious food, while many farmers and packers may have surplus food that can help ease the burden.

How: The Florida Association of Food Banks' food recovery initiative, Farmers Feeding Florida, was established to combat this issue. Across our network, we have refrigerated storage facilities to process donations as well as a fleet of more than 160 refrigerated trucks to safely transport and distribute it statewide. Our Food Bank employees and volunteers are trained and certified in proper food-handling procedures to ensure the quality of produce donations.

What: The funds allocated by the Florida Legislature to the Farmers Feeding Florida program go directly to farmers and packers throughout our state to rescue and distribute wholesome and cosmetically blemished produce to our neighbors in need. The initiative helps Florida farmers offset out-of-pocket costs for packing materials enabling them to scale up donations to multiple truckload quantities.

Another key piece of your preparation is to have a strategic briefing kit prepared before conversations begin. It should include information on your organization or coalition, high-priority issues, and three or four key facts or statistics.

CONTENTS OF BRIEFING KIT

- overview of organization or coalition

- white paper on advocacy issue

- testimonials from advocates and other thought leaders

- recent key news articles that support the issue

- website or social media information driving readers to learn more

Your briefing kit should also include your story. How do you get to a compelling story? I use what I call the "Ronald Reagan Rule": a good story has more impact than a good fact. You need to make sure your participants in these meetings each have a personal story to tell and that the story is also included as a testimonial in the briefing kit. Elected officials hear twenty, fifty, one hundred-plus issues a day, and what stands out to them are two things: (1) how your issue directly affects their constituents, and (2) whether there is an emotional tie they can make with your issue to determine if they should support it or not.

BUILD RELATIONSHIPS

Don't go into a meeting expecting a legislator to make dramatic, sweeping changes in legislation. Think *one*: have conversations about one topic, one issue, and one solution. That's it. If there are other interests or concerns or programs, those topics need to be reserved for a different meeting. So go in and be very clear on what you expect of your engagement with the elected official.

The goal is to build a long-term relationship with your elected official; you want him/her to think of you as an important resource. Before the need to change public policy becomes urgent, you should establish a working relationship with your elected official.

I have a passion for health care issues, and all seem to come back to ensuring the patient has access to the care and medicine they need at the most appropriate time. We had the opportunity to work with a woman whose quality of life was seriously impaired for a full year due to an insurance company issuing over fifty denials to receive a necessary medication prescribed to her by her physician. She testified before policymakers for several years, but she gained little traction.

A year later, we were listening to a committee meeting and a policy-maker said, "Do you remember the woman with over fifty denials? We need to make this change." Months had passed since she testified, but her story remained at the forefront of the issue. It is so important to establish these relationships and repeat, repeat, repeat those stories. One impactful personal story or fact that demonstrates the impact on the individual can be incredibly powerful.

One way to begin building relationships with elected officials is to invite them to come see your facilities for themselves. Invite them to come to special events where you can show them, in person, the positive impact your group is having or that it could have if some policy changes were made. Show them a vision of the future.

Other ways to engage elected officials on issues that pertain to you is through digital/social media opportunities, public meetings, and other platforms. Use these resources to connect so that when you meet with the policymaker on your particular issue, you're not getting to know each other for the first time.

Your working relationship with your elected official must be extended to that person's staff; key staff members are very influential in public officials' decision making. Look for opportunities to build relationships and hold meetings and conversations with staff members before you actually speak to the elected official.

We like to think our elected officials have very global perspectives, but in truth, they're most interested in what affects their home district. So when setting up meetings or communicating with them, let them know that you are a constituent and that they are going to have the opportunity to engage in conversation about something that will have an impact at the local level.

Too often, people begin a conversation expecting the elected official to know what they're talking about. Here are a couple of examples of some of the biggest mistakes that are made once the meeting has been set:

- The first one is to begin by trying to overeducate the elected official. Elected officials don't have time to become content experts on every single issue that they're going to work on. You are the content expert bringing a unique perspective to the conversation. So don't overwhelm a legislator with a lot of technical details. Two or three very good supporting statistics are great. Provide those.

- Another mistake is using a lot of acronyms and jargon; people in health care, education, information technology, or environmental arenas are especially guilty of this. Outside of your day-to-day contacts in your field, few people understand the words and the jargon that you're using. So be very cognizant of that and clear when speaking to anyone about your issue.

Also, don't try to use retaliation to get your way, with threats such as, "Well, if you don't support me, then I won't support you in the future." Shaping public policy means different perspectives coming together and conversation taking place, and the result needs to be a win-win for everyone. Your goal is to establish a positive relationship, and threats aren't going to help you there.

THE CONVERSATION

The way to have the conversation with elected officials is to first clearly outline what the problem is. Second, talk to them about the solution. End the conversation by telling them what you expect out of their engagement. For example, do you want them to support (or not support) passage of a certain bill, or do you just want them to monitor an issue? Be very clear about your expectation of their role.

In your conversation, always talk about your issue from a personal perspective. Again, people want to feel a connection, and when you have a chance to say how the issue affects you, an elected official can understand how it might affect other people in his/her district. So talk about your experience, background, and passion for why this public policy needs to be addressed.

I was conducting an advocacy training to help a group frame their experiences to ensure they were effectively communicating their story. The first person in the group to share his story spent five minutes giving an historical perspective and other points of his situation. I asked him to tell me in one sentence the impact that the policy would have on him personally. The advocate went back to his table and spent a few minutes scribbling on paper before sharing. In one sentence, the advocate had the entire audience in tears. Five minutes of conversation can be replaced by one strong, emotional sentence on the personal impact of policy.

Ahead of time, send a confirmation of the meeting. Don't just be there on time; arrive at the meeting early. Be respectful of the elected official's time. When the meeting ends, thank the official for his/her time, and then, within twenty-four hours, thank the official again, in writing.

In summary, the whole point of advocacy in affecting public policy is that you have an understanding of the issue, and you're able to communicate that understanding to your elected official, who can then understand why and how the issue will affect constituents and exactly how your proposal will bring a solution. And don't forget to tell your elected official how they will be recognized, rewarded, and acknowledged for supporting your public policy initiative.

CHANGE TAKES TIME

When working to affect public policy, remember that while this issue may be your highest priority, elected officials, on a daily basis, have hundreds of other individuals thinking the same way. They are approached by dozens and dozens of organizations requesting their issues have the highest priority.

As a result, public policy is often not shaped in a matter of a meeting or a day or one legislative session or even in one calendar year. Think of your advocacy efforts to influence public policy as being a multi-year activity. It may be that in the first year, you're educating and creating the groundwork to have others accept the idea that change needs to take place. In the second year, you build additional advocates to support your idea, create partnerships, and develop relationships with other policymakers who wish to work with you to communicate the need for this public policy change. And then, sometimes, it takes a third year, or beyond, to acquire all the votes needed to make the change.

Every public policy request is different. While one change may take three months of advocacy efforts and be passed in one session, you may be working on another effort for three years and see little, if any, movement. Some issues, such as global warming, can only be chipped away at while others can be solved more quickly.

This is why it's so important that you build these networks and coalitions. The more diverse the individuals and groups that are coming together are—all under one uniform brand—the more powerful that message will be. When elected officials believe that a significant number of their constituents think a certain issue is a real problem they need to address, that issue tends to rise to the top of the to-do pile. That's why it's so important to do all that preparatory work of building the brand, developing the key messages, conducting the research, and bringing in nontraditional allies.

Again, recognize that diplomacy is important. Advocates can have a disagreement on a particular issue and may be on opposite sides of the coin on a single issue, but they may be aligned and working together on a future issue. So be careful not to burn bridges, because you never know whom you need to have as your friend for future activities.

We're seeing the growing power of caucuses within governing bodies, and you need to make sure that your issue is well communicated to them. Their engagement is very important as you work to build the number of people who are willing to support your public policy. Make sure your issue has a diverse face and that you're telling the story from all of the unique perspectives. Everyone's vote counts!

THE IMPACT OF LEADERSHIP

The impact of leadership on public policy decision making cannot be overstated. You must recognize the power that leadership has. Whether it's a speaker of the house or the chairman of a key committee, these individuals have the power to see to it that your bill or issue is heard (or not), and they have the power to suggest to their colleagues which way to vote.

When setting up meetings with policymakers, ensure you reach all the key people who can affect the decision pertaining to your public policy issue.

For example, if your issue has a monetary ramification, the chair and members of an appropriations committee are, certainly, very important. Map out who needs to be contacted, and prioritize the order in which you are meeting with those individuals so that a key conversation doesn't slip through the cracks. This also helps ensure that those concerned know the value they bring to addressing this public policy issue. Elected officials need to know their time is appreciated and that they are critical to success.

Public officials value the input these coalitions, these constituents, bring to them. But they also know that these advocates are voters, and so they want to know what issues they should be addressing. As an advocate, you bring value to the conversation, so you want to be seen, long-term, as a resource for your policymakers. Let them know to contact you with questions. You want them to know you will regularly communicate with them on new research or new data that may be associated with your issue. They need to see you as a resource as much as you see them as a resource.

ACTIVATING CHAMPIONS

A coalition is only as strong as its member engagement. Members of a coalition need to have something to do; inactivity is a death knell. Once the advocacy plan has been determined with its goals, objectives, strategy, and approved tactics, advocates are ready to be activated. Building champions, at times, may seem like making sausage: not a pretty process, but the end product will be pretty darn good.

A great example of strong member engagement that regularly rallies for a cause is the American Nurses Association, an organization representing the interests of some 3.1 million professionals.[34] This organization exists to ensure policymakers do not ignore the interests of nurses because, oftentimes, those responsible for making

---

34 American Nurses Association, "Policy & Advocacy," accessed December 29, 2015, http://www.nursingworld.org/MainMenuCategories/Policy-Advocacy.

the policies do not understand what it takes to care for patients at their bedside.

The organization successfully facilitates important discussions between its members and legislators at the local, state, and national levels. It empowers members by providing the resources and vehicles they need to engage, and it continually reminds members that their voices need to be heard. Each year, during National Nurses Week, the organization focuses its outreach efforts on a particular theme; the focus in 2015 was on ethical practice and quality care, two big issues in the nursing industry.[35] Nurses' advocacy engagement continues to influence public policy issues in a positive way.

As a recap of this chapter, the following are my recommendations to successfully activate your champions:

- *Be realistic.* Remember that your champions want to do a good job, but you need to be realistic with your advocacy goals. Setting expectations with your internal and external stakeholders is essential. Most advocacy efforts are multi-year projects because if the issue were easy to resolve, it would have been by now. Especially when looking to change public policy, your goal should be to influence your elected official's decision on a specific piece of legislation—not to demand unrealistic, dramatic, and immediate changes.

- *Be prepared.* Before conducting any advocacy effort, you must do some research. Look at the websites, Facebook pages, Twitter feeds, and other social platforms of

---

35 American Nurses Association, "2015 National Nurses Week," accessed December 29, 2015, http://www.nursingworld.org/HomepageCategory/NursingInsider/Archive-1/2015-NI/Mar15-NI/2015-NNW.html.

those you are trying to influence. Know what issues are important to them and whether your issue aligns with their priorities. Make sure you have prepared your materials prior to setting up any meeting. Your materials should tell a compelling story, highlight supporting facts, and clearly define and articulate success. Recognize your opponent's arguments and have strong points to counter them. Your champions should be well versed on the issue and able to communicate the importance and value of addressing it.

- *Be respectful.* It is important to meet regularly with those whom you are trying to influence, keeping your issue on their radar without being abusive or intrusive. Visiting them on their home turf is important. Sometimes, it has a greater impact. Whether it is the district office of an elected official or the high-rise office of a CEO, be respectful of the time requested for your meeting. It should last fifteen to thirty minutes. And holding a loud, disruptive rally outside an office before candid and useful conversations are held is not helpful. Once you have arranged a meeting, send a brief, written note or e-mail, confirming the date, time, place, and topic of discussion. Remember that discussing your position with key staff members can be just as important as discussing it with the top executive or policymaker.

- *Be accessible.* You want to build long-term relationships that will make you a valued resource of information on important issues, both now and in the future. Get to know the folks whom you are trying to influence in different settings. Encourage your organization to invite them to visit your offices, tour facilities, and attend events. Look for positive opportunities such as open houses, annual meetings, or receptions they can attend and possibly speak at.

- *Be liked.* Everyone needs to hear from stakeholders: employees, friends, business associates, or customers. But no one likes a bully or a know-it-all. Don't lecture individuals with technical details or too much information. They need enough to make an educated decision, not become an authority. Make sure you can effectively communicate your position in about three to five minutes. If they need additional information, you can provide that to them in a briefing paper or send them to your website. You should regularly ask the question, "How can I help you?" Know that being helpful is part of being likeable. They can be a valuable asset in communicating and advocating for you. Provide them with additional material on your issue, and invite them to use you as a trusted, knowledgeable resource.

- *Be assertive.* Remember that people are busy. They will only have a few minutes to focus on you. Determine your one, most important issue and get right to the point. This is not the time to bring up lots of issues. As with most individuals, the first and last thing they hear is what they remember. Remember that a story has more impact than a fact. Talk about the issue from your personal point of view.

- *Be professional.* Compromise is part of the process. You should be appreciative and respectful of the effort. You cannot say thank you enough for the time, leadership, and service that your champions and stakeholders are giving to influence the cause. After meeting with key opinion leaders, publicly acknowledge them at meetings, in the media, and in their local district. Proper etiquette means sending a thank-you note and attaching any requested follow-up information within twenty-four hours of any meeting. Whether your stakeholders are aligned with your agenda or not, you want to become a long-term, trustworthy facilitator and convener for the issue.

While this chapter focused on the importance of advocacy engagement to influence elected officials, oftentimes advocacy campaigns are coordinated concurrently with a lobbying team to bring additional expertise, relationships, and navigation as the legislation moves through the process.

Lobbying as a complimentary effort to advocacy can be valuable, especially if the goal is to change public policy. There are times a campaign can succeed with advocacy alone, and other times an effort can succeed with lobbying alone. And sometimes, lobbying and advocacy can work hand-in-hand for ultimate success.

Additionally, it is critical to understand the federal and state laws surrounding advocacy and lobbying engagements to ensure compliance. The definitions of advocacy and lobbying vary from state to state, so it is important to be sensitive to the laws of your state and act in accordance with the local guidelines.

Bottom line, your ability to create and mobilize champions is critical to the success of your advocacy efforts as you work with the real influencers: policymakers.

THREE KEYS TO UNLOCK YOUR ADVOCACY SUCCESS

🔑 Focus on building a relationship with your elected officials.

🔑 Provide advocacy training to the individuals directly engaged with elected officials.

🔑 Provide a concise, clear, and compelling message.

CHAPTER 7

FOSTER (DON'T FEAR) THE USE OF DIGITAL MEDIA

Technology is nothing. What's important is that you have a faith in people, that they're basically good and smart, and if you give them tools, they'll do wonderful things with them.
—Steve Jobs

D igital media, including social media, has revolutionized our lives and the way we interact. It is essential that we engage on these platforms for advocacy efforts; digital advocacy can be a key component in mobilizing supporters to take action with you.

This revolution has also been seen on Capitol Hill. Senators and representatives are more inclined to use social media than they were in the past, which has improved communications and relationships between constituents. We have also seen social media from constituents being influential to senators and representatives who were undecided on an issue.

Digital technology offers a plethora of opportunities to contact, inform, and mobilize a group of citizens. The advantage of digital media is threefold: (1) you can reach a wide and diverse audience quickly, (2) there is minimal cost to setting up these platforms, and (3) they offer you the ability to monitor and instantaneously react to opportunities and challenges.

The first step in utilizing digital media for advocacy initiatives is to create a three-point strategy:

1. Set your goals and objectives.

2. Identify the audience you would like to reach.

3. Prioritize the digital media platforms on which you plan to focus.

Research various platforms to see who is currently involved in your issue, and assess which tools they are using most. Spend some time to see which platform is best to use in reaching and engaging with your audience. One of the most powerful digital advocacy tools is a website. A user-friendly, well-branded website helps increase the reach and effectiveness of advocacy-related communication and mobilization efforts. This central location of resources will work as a hub and spoke with your social media channels to inform and engage audiences to action.

In this digital age, using online resources is key to recruiting thought leaders for your advocacy initiative. Your stakeholders are reading, listening, and conversing on various platforms. And for policymakers, in some cases, voting decisions are based on what thought leaders say on social media.

So what are thought leaders? They are individuals with influence over an audience. The goal is to identify, recruit, educate, and activate the influence of these thought leaders for your issue or cause. You can measure this thought leadership on social media platforms by measuring the increase in conversations about your issue that the general public has and that individual thought leaders have with their followers. Look to see if additional targeted stakeholders are now more engaged in the conversation because of your activities. Use assessment tools to see what resonates and what does not.

A CONVERSATION WITH DIGITAL THOUGHT LEADER SCOTT MONTY

One of the great thought leaders in digital media is Scott Monty. He is an internationally recognized leader in digital communications, digital transformation, social media, and marketing. As principal of Scott Monty Strategies, he counsels brands and agencies on strategy, executive communications, influencer management, the customer experience, and digital initiatives.

Scott spent six years at Ford Motor Company as a strategic advisor on crisis communications, influencer relations, digital customer service, innovative product launches, and more. He also has a decade of experience in communications and with marketing agencies where his clients included IBM Healthcare and Life Sciences, Coca-Cola, American Airlines, T-Mobile, GE Software, and more.

I had the great opportunity to interview Scott about his insights on social media. We had a dynamic conversation on everything from trends and pitfalls to measurement and the future of social media, a topic about which he jokingly stated, "Have we established that it is more than just a fad yet?" I know you will enjoy these points of wisdom and must-dos (and don'ts) about social media.

Me: What role does social media have in advocacy?

Scott: There's no question that social media is a key element to advocacy. It can be the engine that helps to drive advocacy, and the content that you share with your advocates is the fuel. I don't see that changing any time soon because what is social media but just people talking to people? And in some cases, it's people talking to people at scale.

You're going to have different levels of advocates all over the place. When I was at Ford, we talked about the pyramid structure of influencers at the top, advocates in the middle, and then fans at the very bottom. The model shows that your fans are the most loosely affiliated with you, your advocates are those that will do something when asked, and your influencers are basically advocates with audiences.

Me: What is an example of an organization that does advocacy through social media?

Scott: I'm going to look at this through the lens of content. I think Red Bull has been a remarkable example of a company that "gets" its customers. All too often, brands are so excited about whatever it is that they're doing, launching, or announcing that they just blast the message out, whether it's to employees or to customers. It's basically the human version of billboarding. It's getting up there and thumping their chest.

What Red Bull has done online and in print is create life-style content. Red Bull understands what its most passionate customers want and what they do with their lives. And it connects with them via that kind of content. As a result, Red Bull ends up having some of the most ravenous and rabid fans, simply by virtue of those fans being excited about what they're seeing. Red Bull doesn't even need to ask them to do anything. It simply creates the content that fuels this kind of activity.

I can't think of a better way to exemplify exactly what you want advocates to do than to simply give them what they want, and to think the way that they think, and to speak the way that they speak.

Me: Tell us about some of the trends in digital/social media.

Scott: We've seen a rise and domination by Facebook; it's here, and it's currently one of the most important social networks, with a billion people logging in each day. As dominant as it is, it's still trying to outdo Twitter and its real-time data/feed. Facebook is where you go for what's happening with your friends now and in the past twelve to twenty-four hours. Recently, we've seen Facebook trying to be more Twitter-like in reaching out to journalists, who use Facebook as a resource for the content and feed they curate on Twitter. Just recently, Twitter was becoming more like Facebook, but by its nature, Twitter has a bit of a traction problem. The launch of Twitter Moments has brought us more of a curated news destination where people can interact with the content on their own network.

It's an interesting time right now, where the social networks are trying to out-fox each other and trying to be everything. But what we're also seeing is the applications that are more focused in their use actually get better engagement. For instance, it seems like every week people are saying something like "Teens are fleeing Facebook; they're going to Instagram; they're going to other apps." The bottom line is they're still on Facebook, but the reason that their attention is being taken by those other apps is because they serve a purpose. That's why Facebook carved off Messenger as a more robust, standalone app that offers that private kind of interaction that a lot of teens are looking for.

Another example is Instagram; even though it's owned by Facebook, it is still very much a standalone app. Sure, you can post your Instagram photos over to Facebook in a fairly seamless way, but Instagram still acts on its own.

So even though these platforms are bulking up to do everything and serve everyone, they're also diversifying at the same time. And whether it's with Google or Facebook, diversification is really in the cards, and they're serving such a large population that people can pick and choose within that ecosystem which apps actually make sense for them.

Me: What opportunities are you seeing with LinkedIn?

Scott: LinkedIn, in particular, has really upped its game with regard to content. LinkedIn used to be the place where you went to just network with other people; it was shorthand for "my electronic resume," if you will. It really didn't serve as much more than that.

In the last few years, LinkedIn has really doubled down on the influencers: it created a group of about five hundred influencers ranging from someone like Richard Branson to Beth Comstock, the vice chair of GE, to my friend Frank Eliason, who did customer care for Comcast and Citibank. And these opinion makers are basically using LinkedIn as a blogging platform, as another place to share their perspective.

It seems like LinkedIn recognized the power of that and pretty quickly made that functionality available to every LinkedIn user. So now when you go on the site, you have an option of posting an update or sharing a link like you would on other platforms but also of writing some kind of longer-form content. That's designed to make LinkedIn more sticky, so people will stay on the platform longer.

Me: Any thoughts on trends when it comes to social advertising across platforms?

Scott: Recently, I think we've seen that, really, advertising is no longer just nice to have—it's absolutely a requirement. There's a variety of ways that we have to advertise on these networks, and they all have their different product offerings. But it's essentially the same thing where you're taking some piece of content—it could be a video, a captioned image, or a link to your site with some sort of description—you pay money, and it gets plastered in front of people.

I'm going to step on the soapbox for a minute here. The problem I have with the way that social advertising is done is that it's founded on a twice-broken model. Let me explain what I mean by that.

Mass media, mass advertising, first came to prominence in the middle part of the twentieth century. Radio and television were the dominant forms, but certainly outdoor and print have been with us for a long time. And what you had was a way to get creative in front of many more people at a single time than you ever had before.

As we moved into the digital age in the late eighties, early nineties, and beyond, that model was simply transported to the digital space. So billboards, for example, in the digital space are literally the old-billboard model. Even what we watch on YouTube now is akin to a thirty-second spot. Sometimes it's truncated down to just a few seconds, but we're still watching commercials. So really, we were using a model that was already outdated when we came out of the mass-media era into digital. Then we move into social, where people are really trying to connect with other people; it's still a model that was already broken but just plopped down on top of that space. No wonder people are going nuts over ad-blocking technology now and making a big deal about how they remove these ads from their Internet experience, whether it's mobile or desktop based. People simply don't want that kind of interruption anymore.

I'm going to step off of the soapbox now and say that the audience-measurement tools, and more importantly, the audience-customization tools that the social networks give us to work within their platforms today are better than ever. Whether it's Twitter, Instagram, Facebook, YouTube, and now Gmail, you now have the ability to take your e-mail database and plug it into any one of these systems and directly serve ads or content to only the audience that you want it to hit. Advocacy campaigns are capitalizing on this micro-targeting tool.

So you're not doing a spray-and-pray anymore. You're targeting it specifically at people who are or aren't part of your newsletter database or people who are within a certain age category or are not. Again, these are ideal for advocacy efforts.

And there are so many tools now that are unlocked simply by having the good, old-school e-mail address. It seems counterintuitive as things advance, but e-mail, I think, is still and will remain a very important tool for us because of the ability to personalize it. What better way to reach a target audience with a specific advocacy message than through an e-mail sent directly to them?

Me: What company has used social media to pass or defeat legislation?

Scott: Uber is one company that's done this really well. Uber really pushes the envelope where legislation or regulations are concerned. The reason that people are so unabashedly supportive of Uber is that it's a really good service. It's clean. It is predictable. You can open an app and see where your car is in real time, which leaves you assured when and where your ride will arrive.

That kind of customer experience lets Uber turn to its fan or customer base when, for example, it's having trouble with legislation. Uber can reach out to this fan and customer base and say, "Hey, we're having trouble in New

York. Here's a link to let the New York Taxi & Limousine Commission know what you think." The brands that have a connection with their customers and that have those advocates—those customers that are willing to fight for them—can go and ask that kind of thing.

Me: What are some of the pitfalls to avoid with a social media engagement?

Scott: The most common mistake that I still see people making is to chase after the platforms. They get enamored with the latest, greatest, or biggest tool. They immediately think they have to have a Facebook page or a Periscope account or whatever the flavor of the week is without stopping to ask themselves a couple of questions: Why are we rushing into this? What's the business or advocacy goal that we're trying to reach?

If you get right down to it, Facebook likes are really not all that valuable. You want people to take some kind of action on your behalf, whether it's sharing a message or signing a name to an advocacy petition, or clicking through to your website, or whatever. A like is just a digital grunt. We become so enamored with chasing after the digital grunts that it derails the whole strategy process.

Understanding how it fits within the larger realm of what you're doing is equally as important. I'm a firm believer that you shouldn't have a digital/social media strategy as a stand-alone. You should have an overall communications, marketing, or advocacy strategy, and digital/social media is merely one way of expressing that. It's really important to revisit that strategy every time you embark on a new tactic or element to the campaign to make sure you're staying true to that strategy and not getting sidelined. So making sure that you're on track with that strategy is equally as important as making sure that the strategy is right to begin with.

Me: The beauty of social is that you have a lot of analytics to work with, but it takes some real diligence to use them. Can you speak to this a little?

Scott: The challenge with analytics right now is that it's a very specialized area of the business. And while it's easy to get people that are very good at communications—and it's easy to get people that are very good at analytics—the real unicorn is the person who is good at both.

I think it's key to simply have employees who are curious, who are always asking why of your strategy, and the results that you're getting. They're also delving down a little deeper instead of just taking data at face value. They want to know what's happening when they spot a blip in the data.

Me: Is content another pitfall? Do people underestimate the time and focus that it takes to develop great content?

Scott: Yes, that's a really big one. There are a couple of things going on there. First, to get back on one of my soapboxes, particularly with our brethren on the marketing and advertising side of the house, we've been using the word *content* as a euphemism for advertising. True content is more along the lines of whatever connects emotionally with your target audience, with your advocates. It could be something as simple as a picture, or it could be as complex as an in-depth interview.

The key is to stop treating content like it's yet another ad to be put out there. Good content requires more of a journalistic type of approach to copywriting and to creation than any marketing team has had exposure to in the past. This is where it's really important that your marketing and communications teams come together because each has a skill set that the other needs. Communication is like a newspaper: it's a never-ending, 24/7 effort. It has deadlines, an editor cracking a whip, people to talk to, facts to check, images to capture, and so on. It is a complex enterprise, and it is much different than getting a designer and a copywriter to get together and review a brief. So do not underestimate the commitment to content marketing that is required in this effort—it is more like a journalistic enterprise than anything.

A friend of mine, Mark Schaefer, wrote a book called *The Content Code,* in which he writes about a phenomenon that we are undergoing simply because of the proliferation of social networks and because of every brand trying to get in front of people. He calls the phenomenon "content shock," like shell shock from the World War I era. We are just inundated with so much content. I'm a big advocate of less is more. I think you should focus on the quality of your content rather than content bombing—just blasting everything out there for dominance. You're looking for that emotional connection with the people that you're trying to reach. If you're doing it at scale with abandon, then you're not going to make that connection.

Me: Any tips for how to measure social media?

Scott: It's early days with regard to measuring social media. Social media is unfairly positioned in that it gets scrutinized more than other practices of communication and marketing. I don't know if it's because it's so new, or if it's because it's potentially more trackable, or what. But it unfairly gets hampered with this notion of return on investment.

Frankly, I think social media is more aligned with communications than it is with marketing because in my experience, it has been more about the upper funnel. It's been about generating awareness, brand building, and creating relationships. What's the ROI of the telephone on your desk? That's a relationship-management tool as well. What's the ROI of putting your pants on every day? It's hard to measure, right? But it's absolutely essential that you do it every day, and there are negative consequences if you don't!

That's not to say social can be excused from being measured, but we have to approach it with a different mentality. I believe the sophistication of the tools and the platforms is going to expand in the next few years. The next generation coming through really needs to be data-driven.

Whether you use paid tools or free tools, I think you need to be comfortable with whatever tools make sense for your business or advocacy goals that you're trying to achieve.

Me: How do you use employees as advocates, and how do you engage them in a social media campaign?

Scott: This is another critical area that I think a lot of brands don't do very well.

Two friends of mine, Chris Boudreaux and Susan Emerick, wrote a book called *The Most Powerful Brand on Earth: How to Transform Teams, Empower Employees, Integrate Partners, and Mobilize Customers to Beat the Competition in Digital and Social Media.* A big part of the book is about working with employees. It's really important that organizations understand how to create an environment of happy employees instead of just trying to come up with "What should we have our employees tweet?"

Making sure you have happy employees is one of the all-time secrets of having happy customers. It isn't rocket science, and it shouldn't be news to anyone. But if a company hasn't created that environment, it's the same as not having a good product and then trying to go out and promote it on social media.

In this case, your product is your employees. They need to feel like they're engaged, they need to feel like they matter, they need to feel like they've got the flexibility to do what they do. Many companies focus too much on social media policies: How can we keep people from doing X or saying Y? They don't think about how they can actually help employees do their jobs better, be more productive, or just be happier. Getting these pieces right means a company will get more exposure by the way employees talk to others about where they work; they will be your best advocate. It's not about strictly talking about the company all the time. It's about putting your employees at the center of what you do and making sure that they feel valued. Then they, in turn, will put customers at the center of what your company does.

People connect with other people. They don't connect with logos or with faceless brands. It's more amenable for an organization to highlight who the people are that are working for it, along with the special work that they are doing and the way that they touch lives and are making a difference in the world.

From the employees' perspectives, making them feel like they are an essential part of the story—which they are—incentivizes them to want to share without you even having to say anything—"Look at me in this video with the CEO." Giving your employees those kinds of experiences, in preparation for your advocacy and your content development, I think is absolutely spot on.

Me: What are some of the keys things to remember when you're planning for social media?

Scott: There is a tremendous opportunity to expand your advocacy reach using social media channels. Know what you want to achieve with each platform; your goals on Facebook may be different from Twitter and LinkedIn. Know whom you're talking to. In conjunction with that, know how those people like being spoken to, or know how they speak. Understand the rules of the road for each community you're involved in.

Where people get into trouble is when they are digital tourists. There is so much going on, and we're expected to have a strategy for every single one of these platforms, and yet we don't inhabit all of them with any degree of regularity. If you feel like you're a digital tourist, make sure that you or someone on your team is taking the time to inhabit that community to truly understand what makes it tick. If you have never been on Reddit before, and somebody says you need to do an "Ask Me Anything" (AMA) on the platform, then you'd better spend some time doing some research there and knowing how the community on Reddit responds to AMAs.

Me: Where do you think social media is going in the next two or three years?

Scott: It's interesting, because I was just looking at the latest Pew Research Center study. Here we are at fifteen years of dominance of the Internet, and they say we're pretty much saturated. According to the study, 84 percent of adults use the Internet, 58 percent of seniors use it (up from 14 percent in 2000), and 96 percent of young adults are online. I think in the next two to three years, we're going to see virtual saturation. The question is—how does this get integrated into our everyday lives? News consumption is going to be absolutely critical. We've seen what Facebook and Twitter—the two dominant social networking platforms—have been doing with regard to news.

Another area of focus is how Facebook is working on augmented reality. We know they've got Oculus Rift in terms of virtual reality, but augmented reality is a little bit different—it's keeping you in the world that you're in and augmenting it. Not long ago I saw in a lab at the New York Times an interactive mirror that has your feed on it as you're getting ready in the morning. It could be as simple as the next iteration of Google Glass that informs you about things that are around you or that gives you Yelp reviews as you're walking by a restaurant on the street, if that's what you're looking for.

That's where this long-heralded, localized, and personalized advertising could come due: when people are walking around, the right offers or right ads or right advocacy effort gets put in front of them with some sort of augmented-reality device. Look at Apple Watch, which has the ability to push microbits of information to communicate with other devices, whether it's our car, our refrigerator, our house, other people—the possibilities are endless.

Wow! Interviewing Scott Monty was a blast. He provided such valuable information about digital/social media—all considerations for how you can build and implement a successful advocacy campaign.

Takeaways from our conversation that are important to remember include:

1. Know your goals.

2. Know your audience and where they spend their time online.

3. Don't be a digital tourist.

4. Don't put all of the stock in ROI. (e.g., What's the ROI of putting your pants on everyday?)

A CLOSER LOOK

Digital media has evolved from a value-added communications medium to an essential component for the growth of your business and success with advocacy engagement.

Successful online strategy will:

- expand reach to target audiences

- improve brand affinity

- forge new relationships with key influencers, including:
  - bloggers
  - reporters
  - thought leaders
  - decision makers
  - policymakers

- increase advocacy success

It is no longer enough to simply have a digital media presence. It has evolved and become part of a larger machine that enhances all aspects of communication and advocacy. Your organization needs to have a strategic digital media purpose and performance.

Specifically, social media has solidified its role in today's advocacy campaigns. Social media platforms ranging from Facebook and Instagram to Snapchat and Twitter are creating communities for direct engagement with stakeholders. Elected officials, advocacy groups, nonprofits, and businesses are all in the game and are even considered behind the times if they don't have a Twitter account.

Experimentation is the name of the game when it comes to social media platforms to reach audiences with an advocacy message. What content motivates your audiences? What do they share? What do they click on? What persuades them to take a more concrete action like signing a petition or calling a congressional office? Conversational content is key with social media, particularly visual content, and smart organizations keep careful watch over which posts perform well for a particular audience segment and advocacy engagement. Successful engagement grows when you do more of what is performing well—in essence, giving audiences more of what they like and want.

THREE KEYS TO UNLOCK YOUR ADVOCACY SUCCESS

🔑 Does your digital strategy focus on your advocacy goals?

🔑 Are you maximizing each social media platform by fully understanding its capabilities?

🔑 Are you listening as much as you are communicating through social media?

CHAPTER 8

ADVOCACY AND CRISIS COMMUNICATIONS

Failure is not fatal; it is the courage to continue that counts.
—Winston Churchill

ADVOCATES ARE A REAL ASSET IN A CRISIS

We've discussed in previous chapters the need to identify and then mobilize your advocates. This is never more essential than in a crisis situation, and your plan should acknowledge and reflect their assets. Your champions can and will provide perspective and ground troops in a crisis situation. When the crisis occurs, a lack of information allows rumors and misinformation to be disseminated. Your advocates can assist in monitoring the situation on the ground and in the media.

At any time, your organization can face a crisis. I truly believe the saying, "Every organization is just one headline away from a crisis."

The origin of the word *crisis* is the Greek word *krisis*,[36] meaning "decision," or *krinein*,[37] which means "decide." However, the general understanding of the word today dates back to the early seventeenth century. College professors lecturing on crisis communication tactics often note that the Chinese expression for crisis, *wei ji*, is a combination of two words: danger and opportunity. While no organization would want a crisis to occur, planning for it is essential. The organization that properly addresses and manages the response from beginning to end comes out of the crisis as a stronger organization.

There are three types of crises:

- *Immediate.* This would be like a national disaster or an emergency situation (a shooting at a college, an earthquake, an act of terrorism, etc.).

- *Emerging.* This type of crisis is anticipated as a problem begins to develops. In this chapter, I'll discuss how you might mitigate an emerging crisis by assessing the situation at the early stage.

- *Sustained.* This is a situation that may linger for years. Examples include environmental disasters, world hunger, poverty, and so on.

---

36 "Online Etymology Dictionary," Online Etymology Dictionary, accessed February 29, 2016, http://www.etymonline.com/index.php?search=crisis.
37 Ibid.

MCG has been hired to provide crisis communication counsel to address issues including the Gulf oil spill, red tide and phosphate disasters, financial mismanagement by hospitals and banks, Health Insurance Portability and Accountability Act (HIPAA) violations, workplace violence, campus shootings, staff layoffs, tainted blood, forest fires—the list goes on.

We have all seen an issue that has been brewing for days or months finally explode onto the media stage and into the court of public opinion. In most cases, this happened because the situation was handled badly. Examples include a car part or a baby swing that should have been recalled because it was found to be defective, yet when the manufacturer knew about the problem, it tried to cover it up. Another example is that of a CEO who knowingly ignored ethical violations by the leadership team until a whistle-blower's revelations led to a special audit and criminal investigation.

However, sometimes, the crisis cannot be anticipated because it is unfathomable. For example, Pepsi had to deal with a crisis situation when false claims were made that syringes were being found in its soft drinks,[38] and Wendy's found itself faced with a similar crisis when a finger was intentionally planted in the restaurant's chili to scam the company for money.[39] In either case, a coordinated and strategic approach to utilizing advocates and advocacy tactics can help an organization manage the crisis and positively influence the outcome.

Whether your crisis is an attack on your brand, a misstep by volunteers in addressing a public policy issue, or any one of a myriad of other concerns, advocacy and alliance development should be integrated in the crisis communications plan. An organization that is

---

38 Richard Lyons, "HOAXES ARE FOUND IN THE PEPSI CASE," *The New York Times*, accessed February 29, 2016, http://www.nytimes.com/1993/06/18/us/hoaxes-are-found-in-the-pepsi-case.html.
39 "Wendy's Knew from Start Story Was a Hoax," USATODAY.com, accessed February 29, 2016, http://usatoday30.usatoday.com/money/companies/management/2005-06-05-insana-wendys_x.htm.

exposed to public criticisms or has a threat to its reputation and its ability to conduct business needs internal and external advocates to amplify the support for the solution, put the issue into perspective, and create a voice for moving past the problem.

An important strategy in a crisis is to tell the truth, tell it all, and tell it fast. If you are proactive and prepare for a crisis, your internal and external champions may actually help you prevent a crisis or at least assist with responses for best-case/worst-case scenarios for dealing with it. Wouldn't you rather do it now instead of under the pressure of an actual crisis?

In the lifecycle of a crisis, your advocates may assist you in several of the facets of your communication to your various audiences.

1. Verify situation
2. Conduct notification
3. Conduct assessment *(activate crisis plan)*
4. Organize assessment
5. Prepare information and obtain approvals
6. Release information to media, public and partners through arranged channels
7. Conduct post-crisis evaluation
8. Conduct public education
9. Monitor events

CRISIS OCCURS

But before you can leverage your advocate champions, you need to be prepared. It is okay to ask for help. Bring in crisis communication and crisis management experts to assist you and your organization; they have experience and perspective you may not have. Whether you are a Fortune 100 company or a small nonprofit, you are better able to handle crises when you have the following six resources:

1. *A crisis-communications plan (CCP) that is reviewed and approved by leadership.* The CCP is a high-level, step-by-step plan of who, what, when, where, and how to engage in a crisis and potential crisis scenarios. It is updated twice annually.

2. *A crisis-communications response team (CCRT) that has designated individuals with clearly defined responsibilities.* Assigning tasks will save time and ensure a smooth flow of action and communication. Your team should have at a minimum the CEO, chief operating officer, and personnel from communications, legal, and human resources representing your internal stakeholders. Your CCRT should include a leadership representative from each of your key coalition partners. However, your CCRT must have one ultimate leader responsible for key decisions.

3. *Plans tested through role-play exercises with internal and external stakeholders.* This will allow the team to vet weaknesses in the plan. The plan should include a standby statement with approved messages; the midst of a crisis is not the time to be creating messages and having

legal and leadership take precious time to approve them. Create a template with blanks to be completed based on the issue. Proactively invest the time to anticipate key questions. Agree on what can and cannot be said about your organization—for example, "HIPAA and privacy must be respected." Monitor everything that's said and written, including social media. Have a system in place to address facts to avoid recirculation of erroneous information. Be sure to address who, what, when, where, why, and how.

4. *One spokesperson.* Having more than one spokesperson may create inconsistent information. The official spokesperson should be media trained and fully educated on the approved messages. The individual should be accessible and have the authority, knowledge, and sensitivity to speak on behalf of the organization or coalition. Spend time rehearsing prepared statements and answers to possible tough questions that may be asked by reporters, and anticipate and practice new questions as the story evolves.

5. *Appropriate positioning or message to address the issue.* This is one of the first responsibilities of your CCRT. The CCRT will make hard decisions based on research of the environment at the time. Generally, it is best when a mistake has been made to admit it up front and begin doing whatever is possible to reestablish credibility and confidence with your internal and external audiences. You can't go wrong with honesty and transparency.

6. *Recognition of the potential positive or negative impact of the media, especially social media, on resolving the crisis.* Major news events show that social media is one of the most important channels of communications to quickly disseminate your message. Be sure to establish a media point person to monitor, post, and react to media activity throughout the crisis. Leverage the technology to reach out with the messages to not only internal stakeholders but also external stakeholders throughout the crisis. Make sure to document the communication so that you can do a postmortem at the end of the crisis.

As part of developing your messages, the CCRT should consider the stakeholders, the landscape/situation, and logistics. In any crisis, they should, at a minimum:

Determine stakeholders.

- Who will be most affected by this crisis?
- How does this affect our internal stakeholders?
- How will the crisis affect current and potential external stakeholders?

Understand the landscape/situation.

- What is the scope of the crisis?
- What information is known to date about the crisis by each of our stakeholders?
- What additional research can be conducted to understand the situation?
- Are our internal and external advocates prepared to engage when needed?

Coordinate the logistics.

- Who needs to be briefed immediately (e.g., board chair, CCRT, etc.)?
- Have we begun monitoring phones, Internet, media?
- What resources need to be activated to communicate to stakeholders and champions?
- What are we doing to prepare for media inquiries and coverage?
- Are we compiling all information to use in a postmortem?

COMMUNICATING WITH YOUR INTERNAL AND EXTERNAL AUDIENCES

To successfully manage a crisis, you should always communicate with internal audiences first including employees, board members, partners, and suppliers, among others. Methods may include posting the message on internal websites, holding briefing meetings, and regular conference calls. Remember that your internal advocates might want to assist but can only be effective if they are kept in the loop.

Communicating with your external audiences tends to be the piece that gets the most attention in a crisis because it has the greatest potential to exacerbate and escalate the problem if not done correctly. When speaking to the media, you should anticipate, lead, and control the interview. Your spokesperson should tell your story or others will—usually emotionally and without adequate facts. Remember only the designated spokesperson should be authorized to officially speak on behalf of the organization or coalition.

Sometimes, in a crisis, the volume of media inquiries seems like a Mount Everest avalanche. Think of media coverage surrounding the downing of Malaysian Airlines Flight 17, the Deepwater Horizon oil spill, Hurricane Katrina, or the Exxon Valdez disaster.

Thinking ahead of time about the questions that might be asked will make your response clearer and more coherent. The following are some of the questions commonly asked by the media during a crisis:

1. What was the cause?

2. Where and when did it happen?

3. Who, if anyone, was harmed?

4. Is the situation under control?

5. What is being done in response to what happened?

6. What can we expect next?

7. What are you advising people to do?

8. How long will it be before the situation returns to normal?

9. Could this have been avoided?

10. Who is conducting the investigation, and when should we hear the results?

No matter the audience you are communicating with in a crisis, remember the following:

- Stick to the facts. Trying to hide, misrepresent, deny, or exaggerate the facts will ultimately fuel the crisis.

- Be truthful and honest, not speculative. Don't be afraid to say, "I don't know" to a question, but promise to find the answer and follow up as soon as possible.

- Address rumors immediately, and correct any false information.

- People first: if a human element is involved, above all else, be sensitive to the people, their families, and friends who are affected.

- Assume everything you say is "on the record." Don't talk about anything you aren't willing to see on the front page of a newspaper.

- Do not seek to minimize the problem; the court of public opinion may think otherwise.

- Do not be in a haste to talk before you have sufficient information to answer obvious questions about the crisis and about what you're doing to resolve the situation.

- Keep a record of all internal and external communication. When the crisis is over, you will want to evaluate your processes and procedures and make appropriate updates and changes to your plan.

ENGAGE AND LEVERAGE YOUR CHAMPIONS IN A CRISIS

Your advocates or champions bring valuable assets and important third-party influence to the table in addressing a crisis. They have unique skills, relationships, energy, and passion. Although it has been said that you want only one spokesperson communicating to the media at the height of the crisis, you should be preparing your advocates for activation.

Your advocates should be engaged in supporting the brand in community activities or on social media. Your organization needs to have a culture of advocacy so that these champions feel a real long-term sense of ownership and pride in supporting the organization or the issue on a regular basis. Engaging them only in a time of crisis does not lend itself to effective advocacy.

We had an opportunity to work with the people affected by the Deepwater Horizon oil spill in the Gulf of Mexico. It was devastating to hear the stories from third, fourth, and fifth generation shrimp and oyster fishermen. During this time, it was necessary to unite the community in telling their stories to the media and elected officials.

Here are some key components to consider for your advocate engagement in a crisis:

- Make sure you have identified your key champions. Know their phone and cell numbers, e-mail, and address.

- Keep them informed on the progress of the crisis by providing them with facts and top-level messages.

- Identify the best vehicles for their engagement: social media engagement, phone calls, letters, one-on-one meetings, print or video statements, rallies, and so on.

- When it is time for them to engage, make sure they understand what they are being asked to do and why it is important.

- Review the messages and role-play if appropriate. Role-playing can be extremely useful in helping advocates stay focused and on message during times of stress.

- Share the successes and challenges of their engagement.

Remember advocates want to make their community and world a better place. A disaster or crisis can be a rallying point for your advocates. The crisis does not have to be an immediate disaster; it can be a problem that needs to be addressed from a long-term public policy perspective. For instance, think about advocates who have engaged in the conversation about environmental issues such as global warming, which has precipitated the melting of mountain glaciers and caused devastating floods; or ecosystems that are being disrupted, as in California, which has been ravaged by wildfires; or the draining of the Everglades in Florida.

Advocates can be the face and voice to bring attention to these broad and, at times, overwhelming crisis issues. Resolution can take place by bringing together a group of passionate advocates to leverage their influence and demand a solution. Believe it or not, sometimes a crisis results in a very positive outcome.

When the crisis is over, recognize and show appreciation for your advocates' efforts. Some examples include awards (e.g., plaques and certificates), appreciation lunches or dinners, recognition in your organization's newsletter, stories about them placed in the local media, acknowledgment on social media, or calling them out in a speech.

As you can see, a crisis situation is where you will really see the value of having worked so hard to build a base of champions. This is an army that's waiting to help you in times of need. These advocates must feel empowered to help you resolve the crisis and move the organization forward. If you've trained and equipped them, they will, in most cases, want to be a part of turning a negative into a positive; they will want to be a part of making sure that your brand stays strong and continues.

THREE KEYS TO UNLOCK YOUR ADVOCACY SUCCESS

- Do you have a crisis-communication plan?

- Who will be your key spokesperson in a crisis?

- What lessons did you learn from your last crisis?

CHAPTER 9

MEASURING SUCCESS

Feedback is the breakfast of champions.
—Ken Blanchard

I n the business world, you often hear people say, "If you can't measure it, you can't manage it." This is certainly true. You need to quantify and validate the results of your efforts to be able to reinforce and evolve your brand and refine your approach. Having the data helps set the course to measure success against the defined goals and objectives for your advocacy engagement and activation.

No matter the size of your organization or coalition, you can't afford to invest resources in strategies that can't be measured.

What exactly is advocacy measurement and evaluation? Basically, it is any and all research designed to determine the relative effectiveness or value of what is done in advocacy engagement. In the short term, advocacy measurement and evaluation involves assessing the success or failure of specific advocacy programs, strategies, tactics, or activities. This is accomplished by measuring the outputs, outtakes, and/or outcomes of those programs against a predetermined set of objectives. In the long term, advocacy measurement and evaluation involves assessing the success or failure of much broader advocacy efforts that seek to improve and enhance the relationships that organizations maintain with key constituents to achieve an advocacy goal.

Planning for measurement and evaluation should occur at the start of an advocacy effort, ideally while the strategy is being developed or soon thereafter. This is based on the proven premise that evaluation can be a key resource when integrated into advocacy efforts because it supports and informs the work as it evolves. Here are some elements that are important to measuring advocacy success:

- Establish clear, strategic, and tactical goals, as well as desired outputs, outtakes, and outcomes before you begin to provide a basis for measurement of results.

- Differentiate between measuring outputs, outcomes, and outtakes.

- There is no simple, all-encompassing research tool, technique, or methodology that can be relied on to measure and evaluate advocacy effectiveness. Usually, a combination of different measurement techniques is needed.

- Advocacy effectiveness can best be measured if an organization's key messages, key target-audience groups, and desired channels of communication are clearly identified and understood in advance.

- Advocacy measurement and the evaluation process should never be carried out in isolation by focusing only on the advocacy components. Wherever and whenever possible, it is always important to link what is planned and accomplished through advocacy to the overall goals, objectives, strategies, and tactics of the organization as a whole.

It is important to analyze how the measurement and evaluation will be used. Oftentimes, it is used to establish accountability, inform decision making, or encourage local or national learning.

Accountability generally aims to determine if a relationship can be established between an advocacy effort and its observed results. Evaluations that examine the link between advocacy efforts and their results have adopted a standard of contribution over attribution. *Contribution* means determining if a case can be made that advocacy efforts played a meaningful role in producing their intended results.

Informed decision making helps organizations or groups learn in real time and adapt their strategies to the changing circumstances around them. It is an essential part of the ongoing advocacy strategy to be integrated throughout the decision-making process.

Local and national learning generates knowledge that will be useful to individuals beyond those who are involved with the advocacy effort. However, replicating whole advocacy strategies is not advisable, because what worked in one geographic area or political context is not likely to work the same way in another.

OUTPUTS, OUTCOMES, AND OUTTAKES

For advocacy campaigns, you need to consider three areas: outputs, outcomes, and outtakes.

MEASURING OUTPUTS

Measuring outputs is at the bottom of the pyramid. It is the low-hanging fruit. It is generally what is looked at first when assessing the success or failure of a campaign. Outputs count the development, distribution, or deployment of tactics.

Examples of outputs measured include:

- advocates recruited to participate

- letters and calls generated

- e-mails generated and open rates

- meetings held between advocates and key targets

- attendees at an event

- speaking engagements

- articles written

- editorial-opinion pieces (op-eds) or letters to the editor published

- interviews scheduled and conducted

- media hits (TV, radio, and print)

- "followers" or "likes" on Facebook and LinkedIn sites or retweets on Twitter

- hits to the website or landing page

- tools (materials) created and distributed

MEASURING OUTCOMES

The next level on the pyramid is outcomes. This measures whether the tactics listed in your outputs activities generated messages that resulted in any opinion, attitude, and/or behavior changes from the stakeholders you targeted. Did your advocate effectively communicate the message? Did the target understand both your message and the *importance* of the message?

For example, if your output measurement was the number of e-mails sent to the legislative target, your outcome would be based on how many of the e-mails were opened and whether the individual valued receiving the e-mail and understood both the message and the urgency of your issue. This can be difficult for small organizations to measure because oftentimes they don't have the tools or resources to effectively quantify the results.

Some typical examples of outcomes:

- Replies back to your e-mails reflected an understanding and appreciation for the issue.

- Your collateral materials were read by the key targets and generated action.

- The organization's spokesperson has been positioned as a thought leader.

- The events generated additional key meetings because of the increased awareness of the importance of your issue.

- The op-ed spurred a series of articles on your issue and exposed the topic to a wider audience.

- Viewers to your website took action and downloaded information or a form.

- Articles accurately reflected or contained your brand messages.

- Engagement on social media goes beyond "likes" to a robust conversation.

- The speaking engagement generated positive feedback.

- The legislative target agreed to join your effort.

MEASURING OUTTAKES

This final measurement is at the highest level or the top of the pyramid; it measures actions taken that positively affect your issue. In advocacy campaigns, this is the most difficult measurement because most advocacy efforts take time (sometimes, years) to generate the outtakes that result in achieving your overarching goals. However, outtakes define ultimate success. For example, one of your outcomes was that an elected official agreed to support your effort. This led to the outtake of his filing a bill supporting your issue.

Some examples of outtakes:

- The conversation on social media was so powerful that the elected official changed their mind on a specific vote.

- Your social media platforms were linked to others, ultimately generating a commitment to form a broad-based issue coalition.

- The overall efforts have changed or had an impact on the public perception of the organization.

- Damage to the organization's reputation was mitigated.

- The downloads of forms from your website generated a large volume that was sent to the key stakeholders, branding the issue as important.

In your measuring efforts, both internal and external stakeholders should be assessed. When establishing your advocacy effort or campaign, goals need to be created with a metric tied to each stakeholder group, and a continuous assessment throughout the advocacy effort should be conducted. Have you moved the needle? Has your influence on the issue been impactful? Have you moved your stakeholders from "against" or "neutral" to "positive" support and engagement with the issue? As the advocacy campaign progresses, you may have to reevaluate and adapt your goals based on the changing environment.

Keep in mind that reporting and reflecting on what is learned from measuring and evaluating a campaign is an essential part of the advocacy process. This reflection is based on both data and experience. Questions that should be considered regularly include:

- What worked well?

- What did not work?

- What could be improved?

- What lessons are drawn for next time?

- What messages resonated with audiences?

THREE KEYS TO UNLOCK YOUR ADVOCACY SUCCESS

How are you currently measuring your advocacy efforts?

Do you have both quantitative and qualitative measurement parameters?

What tools are you using to measure outputs, outcomes, and outtakes?

CHAPTER 10

MAPPING YOUR ADVOCACY SUCCESS

It is not where you start but how high you aim that matters for success.
—Nelson Mandela

The ancient Greeks had two words for time, *chronos* and *kairos*. *Chronos*[40] refers to chronological or sequential time, and *kairos*[41] refers to a time lapse, a moment of indeterminate time in which everything happens. Advocacy efforts need to be conducted at the right time, in the right sequence, and in the right way. It's a journey that requires a strategic plan and approach.

40 "Kairos," Merriam-Webster, accessed February 29, 2016, http://www.merriam-webster.com/dictionary/kairos.
41 "Chronos," Merriam-Webster, accessed February 29, 2016, http://www.merriam-webster.com/dictionary/-chronous.

TEN MISTAKES TO AVOID IN ADVOCACY CAMPAIGNS

First, let me quickly address some final reminders of errors that can significantly derail an advocacy campaign before it gathers any steam.

1. *Lack of a goal.* If you don't know what success is going to look like, you'll never know if you've achieved it. You need to establish clear goals for your advocacy campaign.

2. *No organization.* This reflects not only the infrastructure needed for success but the structure and the framework for how you utilize those assets. Organization is key.

3. *No strong, effective leader.* We have seen many campaigns with compassionate volunteers who don't have enough bandwidth to be effective. You need volume not only in the number of people participating but also the fervor for activities. They must be willing to commit to seeing the campaign through to the end, which could take many years. And that requires strong, effective leadership from those working to ensure that the engine is running on all cylinders. All of the stakeholders must be fully engaged and on message, and they all must know what their roles and responsibilities are. And you must have that key person driving the train.

4. *No depth.* What is the message? What are you trying to achieve? Is it meaningful? Does it really call for a rally? Can people see that it is significant enough to have their time and energy dedicated to going in and being that advocate voice?

5. *Failure to use all of your resources.* We find this often in advocacy campaigns. From the very beginning, the people involved underestimate the opportunities and challenges, along with the resources they need to be successful. Resources are everything from dollars to staffing to technology. They are also about making effective use of all the communication channels and tactics available to make the campaign more comprehensive to reach the targeted audience.

6. *Starting late in trying to address a situation.* We're seeing this more and more. People often think that if they lie low and ignore an issue, it may go away or resolve itself on its own. But with an advocacy campaign, you have to recognize that as the sequence continues, as the domino effect begins, the voices get louder. This is evident in crisis situations. If you don't step in at the right time, at the beginning—fast, accurate, and full of commitment— you've got a real problem. Starting late, when pursuing legislation, can be very defeating. You must start early to build the plan, plant the seeds, and engage audiences if you are going to meet timelines.

7. *Failure to understand your audience.* You truly need to know what your audience thinks. What do they feel? What motivates them? Where do they receive their news? How does that news influence them? Who are the people who can influence them? Having that depth and breadth of understanding of your target audience ensures that the message you create is one that is going to resonate and move your audience to action.

8. *Unwillingness to upset each other.* So often, with advocacy efforts, you've got to step out and take a stand. That may or may not resonate with everyone. But if you expect change to take place, you must be very strong and vigilant in understanding that your champions, your advocates, your evangelists are with you. And it might not be everyone. In fact, in most cases, there's an opposing side that has a different viewpoint. While your advocates are with you, the opposition might be most affected and, ultimately, upset that you have established such a strong effort and voice in creating your advocacy engagement.

9. *No, or minimal, budget.* Some have the belief that if the cause is worthy enough, people will just join and resources (a budget) don't need to be brought to the table. That's just not true. Whether dollars need to be there to support special events or a social media campaign, an advocacy effort must have, from the very beginning, an identified budget and a clear understanding of how that budget is going to be spent: by whom and with a commitment to doing it right. Taking a half step on the budget will only give you half of the success and results.

10. *Lack of a plan.* This is without question the biggest mistake in advocacy. You must decide from the very beginning which concern needs to be addressed and how you're going to resolve that concern with a plan. A plan needs to have a clear understanding of the goals: who is going to do what, when they will do it, why they are going to do it, what the message is, whom they are sending the message to, and a defined expectation of success. That clear plan is going to be the difference between success and failure.

Throughout this book, we've provided the tools and questions you should ask to begin developing your advocacy action plan to propel your organization to the next level. As overwhelming numbers of individuals seek the advice of their friends and family to help them make decisions about issues they will support, organizations are faced with extreme pressure to join in the dialogue. But in an environment controlled almost entirely by consumers, organizations are falling out of sync with audience expectations and preferences: what consumers want, how they connect, and how they make decisions.

As individuals shift to become advocates—from referring products and services to actively taking a stand for an issue—well-designed advocacy programs can build audience engagement. Advocacy is essential to advance and achieve an organization's mission. Advocacy engagement has the opportunity to improve lives, strengthen communities, and advance brands. Advocacy starts with a campaign that creates awareness and follows the communication funnel to being a loyalist.

People receive thousands of messages each day. Think about it. That's a lot of noise equating to a lot of distractions for each of us. Today's organizations will need to build a more authentic, deeper relationship with audiences by truly engaging them to cultivate advocates. An advocate voice is the single most important criterion in making a policy or purchase decision.

Advocacy engagement is a journey for organizations that starts with a need. The ability to make positive change in the world is powered by advocacy. To succeed on that journey, we've created an advocacy roadmap on the following page to help execute your plan. Now that you have the advocacy tools and keys you need to succeed, go and unlock the opportunities that await you!

ADVOCACY ROADMAP
FOR SUCCESS

- Name
- Logo
- Tagline
- Messaging

BRANDING

A AUDIENCE ENGAGEMENT: CHANNELS

GOAL SETTING AND PLANNING

- Advocacy Plan
- 10-Step Approach (See Chapter 2)

DIGITAL SOCIAL MEDIA

EARNED AND PAID MEDIA Television, Radio, Newspapers, Magazines

DIGITAL WEBSITE

EVENTS

AUDIENCE ENGAGEMENT CHANNELS AND FUNNEL

SPEAKER BUREAU

DIRECT MARKETING Emails, Texts, Direct Mail, Letters

- See A & B

- Improving brand health, audience engagement, passing/defeating legislation

- Analyze outcomes, goal achievement to identify best practices

START HERE → **Issue or Need**

RESEARCH

- Stakeholder Mapping
- Qualitative
- Quantitative

TARGET AUDIENCE IDENTIFICATION

- Thinks
- Feels
- Motivates
- Influences

B AUDIENCE ENGAGEMENT: **FUNNEL**

- Analysis of results and goals
- Adjust if needed

AUDIENCE:

KNOWLEDGE
ATTITUDE
BELIEFS

EDUCATE
AWARENESS
CONSIDERATION
CONVERSION
LOYALIST

MEASUREMENT OF OUTPUTS, OUTCOMES & OUTTAKES

RESULTS

POST-MORTEM REVIEW

ABOUT THE AUTHOR

KAREN B. MOORE, APR, CPRC

Karen is founder and CEO of Moore Communications Group. In the twenty-four years since she began the firm, Karen has amassed an astonishing amount of success on behalf of state and national clients. An advocacy expert, Karen has successfully built a vast array of state and national coalitions, impacting important legislative issues. She has shaped conversations surrounding critical patient access policies using a smart mix of grasstops, grassroots, and strategic alliance development efforts. As a collaborator on economic development, health care, and education initiatives, she often serves as a facilitator, bringing various viewpoints together to help form common objectives and unifying solutions.

As an entrepreneur and industry thought leader, she is highly sought after for her integrated communications and crisis communication counsel. Karen has conducted media and advocacy training sessions for Fortune 500 companies, elected officials, and the British Olympic Team. A distinguished public speaker, she has addressed more than 250 organizations on topics such as advocacy, media relations, strategic planning, crisis communications, marketing, and networking.

Karen sits on the board of directors of numerous organizations, and recognition for her work has brought her honors, including the Distinguished Leader Award of the National Association of Community Leaders.

MAJOR CONTRIBUTOR
TERRIE ARD, APR, CPRC

As President of Moore Communications Group, Terrie works on the strategic direction of the firm, including key initiatives, strategic partnerships, business development, and major clients. With a passion for collaboration and culture building, Terrie oversees the firm's account servicing and production teams. She brings to the role more than twenty years of marketing and business strategy experience in a range of industries including health care, education, workforce development, retail, and agriculture.

Terrie is an authority in corporate positioning and branding with a keen focus on strategy and creativity. Her expertise includes crisis communications, communications strategy, and hiring and retaining the best people.

Today, Terrie oversees all areas of strategic growth for the firm. Under her leadership, the firm has tripled in size and received awards for both client work and employee satisfaction.

SOCIAL MEDIA CONTRIBUTOR
SCOTT MONTY

Scott Monty is an internationally recognized leader in digital communications, digital transformation, social media, and marketing.

As Principal of Scott Monty Strategies, he counsels brands and agencies on strategy, executive communications, influencer management, the customer experience, and digital initiatives.

Scott spent six years at Ford Motor Company as a strategic advisor on crisis communications, influencer relations, digital customer service, innovative product launches, and more. He also has a decade of experience in communications and with marketing agencies, where his clients included IBM Healthcare and Life Sciences, Coca-Cola, American Airlines, T-Mobile, GE Software, and more.

He is a board member of the American Marketing Association and an advisor for RPM Ventures, My Dealer Service, Crowd Companies, and Clever Girls Collective. He writes about the changing landscape of business, technology, communications, marketing, and leadership at ScottMonty.com, where he distributes the widely acclaimed *The Full Monty* newsletter.

Moore Communications Group

At Moore Communications Group, we specialize in understanding and connecting with your target audiences—powering you to new levels of business success. From advocacy outreach and innovative digital campaigns to an integrated communications approach, we blend strategic ideas with smart execution to increase your presence, grow your influence, and strengthen your brand's value. Representing Fortune 500 companies and small organizations alike, we get results that drive meaningful action.

Moore Communications Group is headquartered in Tallahassee, Florida, with offices in West Palm Beach, New Orleans and Denver. Learn more about engaging Moore Communications Group as your communications partner at moorecommgroup.com or (850) 224-0174.

"By placing your audience at the center of a multichannel communications engagement, you can create a deeper, more meaningful connection. After all, your audience is in more than one place—and you should be too."
—Terrie Ard, President,
Moore Communications Group